T0267318

Favorite Flies for

YELLOWSTONE NATIONAL PARK

50 ESSENTIAL PATTERNS FROM LOCAL EXPERTS

PAUL WEAMER

STACKPOLE BOOKS

Essex, Connecticut
Blue Ridge Summit, Pennsylvania

This book is dedicated to my many nieces and nephews:
Kylie, Gavyn, Liam, and Dean Weamer; Lily, Emme, Macy,
Kingston, and Katy Baker; and John, Manny, and Gabby DelValle.
I hope I can fish Yellowstone with each of you someday.

STACKPOLE BOOKS

An imprint of Globe Pequot, the trade division of
The Rowman & Littlefield Publishing Group, Inc.
4501 Forbes Blvd., Ste. 200
Lanham, MD 20706
www.rowman.com

Distributed by NATIONAL BOOK NETWORK

British Library Cataloguing in Publication Information available

Library of Congress Cataloging-in-Publication Data available

ISBN 978-0-8117-7076-7 (cloth : alk. paper)
ISBN 978-0-8117-7077-4 (electronic)

♾™ The paper used in this publication meets the minimum requirements
of American National Standard for Information Sciences—Permanence of
Paper for Printed Library Materials, ANSI/NISO Z39.48-1992.

CONTENTS

ACKNOWLEDGMENTS

Thanks to George and James Anderson, Dave Benoit, John Campbell, Michael Delfino, Matt Grobe, Bob Jacklin, Matthew Long, Bucky McCormick, Matt Minch, Joe Moore, Richard Parks, Dandy and Dean Reiner, Walter Wiese, and Rick Wollum for taking the time to share your flies and the stories behind them. I couldn't have written this book without your contributions.

Thanks to Jay Nichols and my editors, Lynn Zelem and Elissa Curcio, at Stackpole Books. Thanks also to Ross Purnell and *Fly Fisherman* magazine.

Thanks to my wife, Ruthann, to whom I could dedicate all of my books. Without her, I wouldn't have written any of them.

Finally, thanks to Edna McConnell. My grandmother passed away at the age of ninety-five on December 12, 2021, while I was working on this book. She was funny, strong-willed, caring, opinionated, and loving. There will never be another person like her, and she had a tremendous impact on my life.

INTRODUCTION

The United States has sixty-three national parks. Many of them offer excellent fishing opportunities for various types of cold-, warm-, and saltwater species. But if there's one park that's synonymous with great trout fishing, it's Yellowstone.

Yellowstone became the world's first national park when it was created on March 1, 1872. But Native peoples and hungry explorers began fishing it for food long before that. I'm currently reading a fascinating book called

The History of Mammals in the Greater Yellowstone Ecosystem by Lee H. Whittlesey and Sarah Bone (Kindle Direct Publishing, 2020), and while that book's primary focus is furry critters—bears, mountain lions, wolves, elk, bison, deer, and others—described in historical writings of mountain men and explorers, there are also discussions of trout and other fish.

The trout that are mentioned are, of course, cutthroat trout, the only native trout in Yellowstone's rivers and creeks. The most common

Yellowstone received the nickname "Wonderland" in the late 1800s as a marketing ploy to encourage tourists to visit. But even today, the park truly is a wonderland. Few places left on Earth offer such diverse and magnificent trout fishing where wild animals and anglers alike traverse beside hot springs, geysers, mud pots, and breathtaking scenery.

species is the Yellowstone cutthroat, but the park also hosts a smaller native population of westslope cutthroat in the Madison River drainage. The only other native fish of importance to fly anglers are fluvial (stream dwelling) and adfluvial (primarily lake dwelling) grayling and mountain whitefish. The park's grayling population is small, though you could encounter one in the Madison and Gibbon River drainages. Efforts are currently being made to restore grayling to more of their historic range.

Mountain whitefish (often called "whities" by anglers) generally get a bad rap: They are salmonids, which means they are closely related to trout and grayling. They look similar to grayling, minus the spots, iridescent blue coloration, and prominent dorsal fin. But a lot of anglers view them as a less desirable species. I don't mind catching whitefish. I learned to fly fish on Pennsylvania trout streams where there aren't any whitefish, so if I have a whitie on the end of my line, it means I'm fly fishing the West, and I like that. And though I sometimes hear anglers compare whitefish to creek chubs (an eastern US fish in the minnow family), whitefish are actually considered a native game species in Yellowstone National Park and protected because of it.

Whities take flies and pull on your line. What's not to like? And for the record, while you can catch and kill some of the other wild, but nonnative, trout species in park waters (regulations vary, so always check the rules for the specific water you're fishing), mountain whitefish, along with their cutthroat trout and grayling cousins, are protected everywhere and must be returned to the water unharmed.

The fly patterns in this book will generally work well for any of the fish you are trying to target in the park, though some were developed for a specific waterway or specific trout species. In addition to the native cutthroat trout I mentioned, you can also find brook,

brown, rainbow, and cuttbow (a cross formed when rainbow and cutthroat trout interbreed) trout, as well as lake trout.

The lake trout are wild descendants of fish stocked into Lewis Lake in 1890 by the US Fish Commission. All nonnative park stocking was halted in the 1950s. Today, lake trout are one of the park's biggest concerns because they have infiltrated Yellowstone Lake and caused its world-famous cutthroat trout populations to crash, though remediation efforts are now beginning to show fruit. This has been accomplished by gill-netting lake trout to kill them and by intentionally destroying their spawning nests (redds).

Park officials also occasionally poison nonnative trout in a stream, or section of a stream, to help restore native cutthroat or grayling fisheries. And in other places, such as Slough Creek, the park has instigated mandatory must-kill regulations for rainbow and obvious cuttbow trout to try to stop them from hybridizing with the native cutthroat. These regulations can change from year to year, so always make sure to read the most current fishing regulations for where you plan to fish. But please give strong consideration to releasing all of the park's trout you are not legally obligated to harvest. If you catch a large fish in Yellowstone, there's a very strong chance that the only reason that fish arrived in your net is because someone who caught it previously put it back. Repay that debt, and leave the trout for the next angler—or maybe even yourself, as your paths could potentially cross again on your next trip.

Before commencing any park fishing trip, you must acquire a Yellowstone fishing permit. The licenses for the border states—Montana, Wyoming, and Idaho—are not valid in the park. You can purchase a Yellowstone fishing permit at many fly shops and general stores outside the park as well as some stores

Cutthroat trout, mountain whitefish, and grayling are native to Yellowstone National Park, and they are all protected by strict catch-and-release angling regulations because of it. The park hosts two species of cutthroat: Yellowstone cutthroat (pictured here) and the less common westslope cutthroat found in the Madison River drainage.

within it. But beginning in 2021, you can also purchase a permit online. I advise buying your permit before you arrive to fish, just so you don't have to search for a vendor after you get here. You can buy your permit from recreation.gov (type "Yellowstone fishing permit" into the home page search box) after you create an account.

Because Yellowstone is such a special place, and very popular with tourist anglers, it has a number of less-common fishing regulations of which you need to be aware. First, even though some of the flies pictured in this book have a barb on their hook, the barb on any fly tied to your leader must be mashed down before you begin fishing. There's a good reason for this: Barbs don't really help you keep the fish hooked, and they can be damaging to a fish's mouth when you try to remove them. You're allowed to have barbed flies in your boxes, but you're not allowed to fish them in Yellowstone. And your flies may get scrutinized to ensure you're following the rules.

My friend John and I were walking out of the Gardner River canyon in the park when he asked me if I'd ever been checked by a fish warden (park ranger) in Yellowstone. I was in the process of telling him that I hadn't when I looked up to see one approaching. The ranger said she was new at her job, but that was obvious to us. John and I had already cut the flies from our leaders before we began the steep hike back to the car, but the ranger demanded to see the flies we were using anyway. I reached into one of my boxes and showed her the crushed-barb fly I had just cut off. She let me go. But John inadvertently grabbed the wrong fly from his box, one with a barb, and showed the ranger. She immediately began a lecture about using barbed

Mountain whitefish are sometimes regarded as a less desirable species by park anglers. But these fish are beautiful, with their forked tails, raspberry-spotted cheeks, and bright, shimmering silver to bronze scales. They take flies and pull on your line, just like trout and grayling.

hooks and gave John a warning, which she recorded in the park's computer system, even though he explained what happened.

John was very unhappy, of course, and his fishing partner didn't make it any easier as he grilled him, while enthusiastically laughing, on what other crimes he may have committed that day. I've heard stories of park rangers sticking an angler's fly into a cotton ball and fining them if it pulls any fibers when it's removed. I've not experienced this, but the lesson here is to make sure you completely mash the barbs on your flies and follow all other park regulations.

Felt-sole wading shoes are prohibited in the park to help stop the spread of invasive species. Anglers are also not allowed to use lead, either on their leader (split shot) or incorporated into fly patterns. Lead is harmful to birds

The park's wildlife proximity regulations help keep humans from getting too close to the animals, but sometimes the animals walk up to you. Here, the author's fish has attracted the attention of a young elk. (photo by Ruthann Weamer)

Grayling aren't common in the park, as competition from nonnative trout species has caused populations to drastically decline or disappear. But there are places where anglers can target them. Park biologists are currently working to restore these beautiful fish to more of their native range.

and other animals when they eat it, so Yellowstone's authorities want to keep it out of the ecosystem. Tungsten weight and brass bead heads are allowed. Most of the fly shops near the park sell lead-free weights, but you probably have no idea if the flies you've purchased include lead or not. If you tie your own, or stick to dry flies, you won't need to worry about that. And you can always ask the people at the shop where you buy your sinking flies if they include lead. They may not always know either, but it's worth a try.

Another rule fairly unique to the park is that you are only allowed to use flies with one hook. Articulated streamers—those tied with two joined hooks—have become very popular, but you're not permitted to fish these flies in the park for the same reason you're supposed to mash your barbs: Two hooks cause more damage to the fish you're about to release than one. If you have an articulated streamer you simply must fish, you can take wire cutters and cut off the bend and point on one of the hooks to be legal. But you won't find any articulated streamers mentioned in this book because of the park's regulations.

One final thought about fishing in Yellowstone National Park. It can be difficult to believe, if you only drive the paved roads, stay mostly in your car, or walk the boardwalks to the usual tourist sites, but this is wild country—as wild as anything left in the lower forty-eight states. There are things here that can hurt or even kill you. Thermal areas can scald you. Bison, mountain lions, wolves, even the deer, pronghorns, moose, and elk sometimes become aggressive near mating season or if they are tending to their young. The park has proximity regulations in place for all of Yellowstone's wild animals: You're not allowed within 100 yards of bears and wolves and 25 yards of basically any other mammal.

You should generally stay even farther away than that. But it's the bears that you need to be the most aware of.

I've had several people tell me that they've been fishing the park since the 1980s and they never carried bear spray then, and they won't do it now. My response is always the same: There are so many more grizzly bears in Yellowstone today than there were thirty, twenty, even ten years ago, that if you haven't fished it since the '80s, we're not really even talking about the same place.

In 2020, my wife and I were fishing the lower end of Slough Creek when we were charged by a grizzly bear that ultimately caused that section of the creek to be closed to the public for a couple weeks. We had unknowingly pushed out a large, charcoal-colored wolf from some willows along the creek about fifteen minutes before we saw the bear. We hadn't noticed the wolf before it ran past us, but we saw the grizzly as it approached from 300 yards on the far side of the creek.

My wife and I froze as the big bruin loomed, glaring at us before it flattened its dark chestnut ears, cascaded down a steep muddy bank, and violently thrashed across the trout water to our side. What we didn't know at the time was that the wolf and bear were headed to those willows for the same reason: There was food in there from a kill. The entirety of our bear story is too long to include in this book. But since I'm writing about it today while my wife is currently making eggs for breakfast, we obviously survived. We did have to pull our bear sprays from their holsters and even remove their plastic safeties. But the bear turned its charge before reaching us, and we, thankfully, didn't have to fire them.

Statistics reveal that fishing the park isn't nearly as dangerous as driving your car to reach it. You don't need to be afraid while you're there. But be aware. Carry bear spray and know how to use it. Don't get so lost in the amazing fishing that you forget to look around, primarily for safety purposes, but also to soak in the beauty. And use the flies from this book, designed by amazingly creative fly tiers, to catch the beautiful wild trout that thrive in one of our world's last near-perfect places.

It's been said that great fisheries drive the development of great fly patterns. Many of the fifty flies I've included in this book were developed specifically for fishing the Yellowstone National Park region. The others, though designed elsewhere, work so well in the park that I decided to include them. My favorite part of writing the book was meeting, or talking on the telephone, with many of the flies' creators and discovering their stories: how they arrived in the Yellowstone region, what they were trying to imitate with the flies they tied, why they believe their flies work so well.

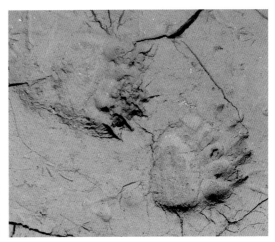

These bear tracks in a muddy bank along Slough Creek, not far from where the author and his wife had their grizzly bear close encounter, are a strong reminder that Yellowstone is a wild place where humans aren't always in control. You don't need to be afraid to fish the park, but you should always carry bear spray and be cautiously aware of your surroundings.

This coyote looked like someone's pet dog as it watched traffic flowing near the park's West Gate, but wild animals are unpredictable and anglers must always keep their distance.

I've loosely organized the book's flies by their order of importance from the beginning to the end of the park's fishing season. But there is a lot of variability with this. The streamers can be fished any time. I've caught park trout on streamers early in the season when the water is still high and off-color, but I've also used them effectively after a summer thunderstorm has roiled the water and even during bright, sunny summer low-water periods, as well as when the park's trout are aggressively feeding in the fall. It's the same for the park's aquatic and terrestrial insects: Yellowstone is huge, and while one hatch appears in a specific waterway, it may be days, weeks, or even longer before it appears in another that's flowing at a different elevation or geographical location.

This is not a fly-tying book, though you'll find the pattern recipes listed if you'd like to tie them yourself. It's a book that showcases the fly patterns that some of Yellowstone's most knowledgeable anglers think you should have with you when you fish the park. But a fly pattern without context isn't all that interesting, so I've included as much information as possible from the people who created the flies. I hope that when you read Dean Reiner's story about fly fishing during his tour in Vietnam, that suddenly his Pink Pookie becomes more meaningful than just another grasshopper pattern; that you feel the enthusiasm in the way Richard Parks, the dean of fly fishing in Yellowstone's northeastern corner, still gets passionate about the difference between a Hare's Ear and a Matt Minch's Bead, Hare, and Copper; and that you recognize that the fly patterns created by Blue Ribbon Flies' Nick Nicklas help keep his memory alive after his life was cut tragically short. There really is more to fly fishing than just catching trout, especially in a place like Yellowstone.

Minch's Joffe Jewel

- **Hook:** #10-12 2XL streamer hook
- **Thread:** Black 6/0
- **Tail:** Red hackle fibers
- **Body:** Silver embossed tinsel
- **Wing:** White marabou
- **Overwing:** Yellow marabou

If you're a fly fisher living outside the Greater Yellowstone Area, you may not have heard of Matt Minch. I didn't know about him until Richard Parks (the owner of Parks' Fly Shop in Gardiner, Montana, near Yellowstone's North Entrance) told me of his importance to Yellowstone National Park fly design. When we spoke on the phone, Mr. Minch told me that he's now retired from production fly tying, but when he was tying for money, it was mostly for "beer money."

It was Minch's Joffe Jewel that intrigued me the most when I first saw it in Parks's shop. I'd been to Joffe Lake before. It's a small lake, more of a pond really, that you access just outside of Mammoth, near the park's northern gate. You have to drive past parked plow trucks, gas pumps, small cabins, and tarped Ski-Doos to reach the lake. In other words, it doesn't really seem like you should be allowed to be there when you're passing through some of Yellowstone's behind-the-scenes infrastructure, but you are.

Matt Minch's Joffe Jewel is a simple, yet very effective, streamer. Yellowstone's pond- and lake-living brook trout love it. But it's also a great fly to try when fishing creeks and rivers for cutthroats, browns, and rainbows during low-water conditions where fish are more likely to eat a smaller baitfish imitation.

The lake is filled with small brook trout, often called "brookies" by anglers. The park's brook trout are descended from fish stocked long ago, before we thoroughly understood how their introduction could damage the ecosystem. In much of their native eastern US range, brookies have been displaced by nonnative brown and rainbow trout. But in Yellowstone, it's brook trout (as well as brown and rainbow trout) that displace native cutthroats. Park biologists are working to eliminate nonnative trout in some waters to protect native fisheries. It's sad to have to kill these wild fish, which are here through no fault of their own, but native fisheries must be protected and restored wherever they are viable or we will lose them, and a huge part of what makes Yellowstone special, forever. That often means that the brookies I sought to protect near my childhood home in Pennsylvania need to be removed in Yellowstone. And I fully support that work.

It was most likely my beginnings as an eastern brook trout fly fisher that drew me to Mr.

Joffe Lake, just outside of Mammoth Hot Springs, is full of brook trout. Most of the fish are small, but they're beautiful and usually willing to eat a fly. Joffe is a great place to visit with children or new fly anglers, or when other park waters are too high to fish during early season runoff.

Minch's Joffe Jewel fly pattern: Like the brook trout I grew up catching, it was familiar. My father learned to tie flies in the 1970s from his friend Steve Campbell, but he didn't tie a lot of different fly patterns. He mostly tied a simple marabou streamer that Steve had shown him. In the 1960s, Minch used the same colors (yellow, white, red) incorporated into the famous hair-wing brook trout streamer, the Mickey Finn, to create his marabou-winged Joffe Jewel. And those colors are the only difference between the Joffe Jewel and the black marabou streamers my dad ties—the first fly my father taught me to tie and the first fly I tied that caught a trout, a small brook trout from a Pennsylvania stream. Different anglers and different waters, thousands of miles apart, yet using the same basic fly concept to catch the same kind of trout. I think that's pretty cool.

Fishing Tactics

When I purchased a couple Joffe Jewels from Parks' Fly Shop to fish and photograph for this book, Richard Parks instructed me to "pitch that thing out in the middle [of the lake] and just let it sink, then strip it back with six-inch strips." So when I arrived at the lake, I did just that. But I didn't get a chance to strip the fly back—a brook trout ate it just after it sank below the surface. I landed and released the fish and cast again. This time I was able to strip once before another brook trout ate it. The same thing happened on my next four casts. I made two casts without hooking a brook trout, so I walked to another spot and proceeded to catch fish on my next seven casts there.

I'm not telling you this to brag about my skill as an angler—brookies aren't known to be a cunning quarry (it's one of their virtues)—but rather to extol the ability of the Joffe Jewel when it comes to catching brook trout in its namesake lake.

- **Hook:** #4-8 3X long streamer hook
- **Bead:** Black brass
- **Thread:** Black 6/0
- **Tail:** Brown barred chickabou
- **Abdomen:** Black flash or sparkle chenille
- **Thorax:** Dark hare's ear Spirit River Squirrel Blend Dubbing
- **Hackle:** Grizzly, dyed brown

Minch's Black Bead Brooks' Stone

Matt Minch told me that he got the idea for his Black Bead Brooks' Stone and his Golden Stone from the well-known stonefly nymphs developed and popularized by American fly-fishing pioneer Joe Brooks. Brooks's contributions to fly fishing through his fly designs, articles, and books are vast, but perhaps his greatest gift to the sport was mentoring arguably the most important fly fisher of all time, Lefty Kreh.

Mr. Minch said that he likes the idea of "tying in the round," which means tying a fly that looks the same on the top as it does on the bottom so as it tumbles through a riffle, it always appears to the trout as it was intended by the fly tier. This idea, endorsed and promoted by Brooks and also popularized by western fly-fishing legend Polly Rosborough through his fly patterns and book, *Tying and Fishing the Fuzzy Nymphs*, isn't as well publicized today as it was in the 1950s and '60s, but it's still just as effective for catching trout.

Richard Parks (owner of Parks' Fly Shop) said that Minch's stoneflies are very popular

Matt Minch's Black Bead Brooks' Stone was inspired by angling legend Joe Brooks. The fly works well during the Salmonfly hatch, particularly if the fish are refusing your dry-fly imitations due to angling pressure or high water.

during Yellowstone's fabled Salmonfly and Golden Stonefly hatches, but he laments the ability to procure some of the necessary materials to tie the flies today, particularly the Golden Stone version. Parks, like many fly tiers and shop owners, is very particular about the color shades used in his shop's flies. Matt Minch agreed with Parks during our conversation about the flies and said that it's very hard to find the brown-olive flash chenille that he prefers for the golden variation. Parks said they have the flies tied with an antique gold–colored sparkle chenille made by Montana Fly Company. The pattern still works, but I got the feeling that Mr. Parks believed it would be even better if he could find the original material used by Minch.

Minch ties his Black Bead Brooks' Stone in sizes 4 to 8 and his Golden Stone in 8 to 12, but Parks said that the middle sizes, 6 for black and 10 for golden, are the most popular. I find that I catch the most trout with large, heavy stonefly patterns like these in deep

The many species of stoneflies that anglers call Golden Stones emerge over a much longer time period than Salmonflies, so the trout get accustomed to seeing them. This makes fishing nymphs, like Minch's Golden Stone, productive for an extended portion of the season.

rivers such as the Yellowstone or in midsized and smaller creeks during periods of high water, or when the water is a little off-color, most often during the end of runoff or after a thunderstorm. During clear, low-water conditions, trout are more readily able to scrutinize large flies and often ignore them. These larger nymphs can also be heavy enough to constantly snag the stream bottom when the water is low, which doesn't allow them to drift naturally; you won't catch many trout if your fly is constantly stuck on a rock.

Fishing Techniques

I generally fish large, heavy nymphs like Minch's black and gold stones beneath an indicator, rather than suspended below a dry fly. Many dry flies aren't buoyant enough to remain on top of the water, particularly in heavy currents, when they have a big nymph hanging from them, though some of the largest Chubbies and other giant stone patterns can be used in this way. Some anglers also prefer to fish these stonefly nymphs with tight-line techniques, forgoing a traditional indicator altogether. This can be effective too, particularly to get the nymphs quickly to the stream bottom where they'll usually catch the most fish. Using a tight-line nymphing method is also a good choice when fishing areas of significantly variable depths (most often found in larger rivers) where an indicator, fixed in a static position, can be less effective for keeping the flies in the fish's feeding zone as the water's depth changes.

Heavy stonefly nymphs can also be used as a split-shot substitute for anglers who are weary of their shot constantly sliding down their leader or falling off (I know I am). Just tie a smaller nymph to the bend of the big stone's hook and allow the stonefly's weight to pull the smaller fly along for the ride to the stream bottom.

Kosmer's Pat's Rubber Legs

- **Hook:** #8 Tiemco 5263
- **Thread:** Black UTC 140
- **Underbody:** Lead-free wire
- **Legs:** White round rubber legs (medium)
- **Body:** Brown/yellow Hareline variegated chenille (medium)

Bill Kosmer is a Pennsylvania fly fisherman who's been traveling to fish Yellowstone's trout waters annually since 2007. He's also a former customer of mine, from my days managing the TCO State College fly shop in central Pennsylvania, who's become a good friend. Since my wife and I moved west, nearly ten years ago, Bill has included me each season in his Yellowstone fishing plans. A lot of anglers get lost trying to fish every waterway in the park, but not Bill. Usually accompanied by his wife Heidi or his friend Brad, Bill generally fishes the same waters each season. Though this lack of wanderlust makes Bill predictable in his fishing pursuits, it also makes him very good at what he does.

Many anglers think of Yellowstone National Park as a dry-fly fisher's paradise, because it is. But Bill isn't necessarily looking for an epic rise that plucks his fly from the surface, though he's happy when that happens. He gives the fish what they want, and that often includes subsurface nymphs. One of his favorite patterns is his take on the famous Pat's

The Pat's Rubber Legs is one of the park's most productive and commonly fished stonefly nymph patterns. Bill Kosmer's version (tied by Bill Kosmer), with its white legs and variegated brown/yellow chenille body, works very well in the park. But on any given day, black, purple, peacock, yellow, and other-colored Rubber Legs can also produce fish.

Rubber Legs nymph. When I asked Bill if I could include "his" pattern in this book, he was quick to point out that he didn't invent the Rubber Legs (that was an Idaho guide named Pat Bennett); his fly is just a color variation. But the Pat's Rubber Legs is also a variation of an even older pattern, the Girdle Bug. This is how fly-tying progression often works. Very few patterns are designed in a vacuum. We all have to start somewhere.

I've witnessed the effectiveness of Kosmer's Pat's Rubber Legs firsthand. Bill and his friend Brad have a unique tradition for fishing a pool in their favorite Yellowstone National Park brown trout stream: They take turns with one rod, using the same fly, and often it's Bill's version of the Rubber Legs. The guys do this every evening for several days. The angling partners fish elsewhere in the morning, but each afternoon they descend a steep canyon to hole up for the evening's fishing. I've gone with them several times, and they really make the place feel like home.

Bill and Brad have a little spot in the stream they call their cooler, where the water eddies just enough that beer cans, chilling in the pristine water, won't float away. There are a couple big rocks the guys call chairs. This is important because while one angler fishes, the idle anglers sit in the chairs and wait their turn. But they don't do this quietly. You see, if it takes you longer to catch one of the many wild trout residing in the stream than the anglers sitting on the stone chairs feel is appropriate, they begin to heckle. It may not be everyone's idea of peaceful, contemplative Yellowstone National Park fly fishing, but it's beautiful for what it is nonetheless.

Fishing Techniques

Stonefly nymphs crawl among the cobbles in most of the rivers and creeks of Yellowstone National Park. They don't swim, so you want them to drift, drag-free, along the stream bottom to effectively imitate them. Most anglers fish these weighted flies in heavy pocketwater or riffles and runs.

It's important to get your fly to sink quickly into the trout's feeding zone before the gushing current rips it over their heads. Nontoxic split shot added to the leader can help. But the shot often gets stuck between rocks and can break off the flies if it's been added above them. You can employ drop-shot rigs (where shot is added beneath the flies) or other methods to mitigate this, but it's often better to use heavily weighted flies. Bill weights his Rubber Legs with lead-free wire, and mentioned that he feels it's necessary to add an extra turn or two of the lead-free wire to equal the weight you'd get by using lead.

Important note: The eddies and rocks that Bill and Brad use for their beer cooler and chairs are in their natural position. You should never move rocks and other natural items in the park.

Bill Kosmer poses with one of the many Yellowstone brown trout that have eaten his version of the Pat's Rubber Legs. On this mid-September afternoon, the fish were aggressively taking Bill's large fly even during low-water conditions.

Parks' Salmonfly

- **Hook:** #2-8 2XL standard dry-fly hook
- **Thread:** Black 6/0
- **Tail:** Brown and black bucktail
- **Body:** Tangerine orange (sometimes called bittersweet orange) acrylic yarn
- **Palmered hackle:** Brown, trimmed to width of hook gap
- **Wing:** Brown and black bucktail
- **Hackle:** Brown

Merton Parks and his family were living in Minnesota during the Second World War when he decided he wanted to learn to tie flies. Merton used a copy of Ray Bergman's book *Trout*, originally published in 1938, to teach himself. His son, Richard Parks, the current longtime owner of Parks' Fly Shop in Gardiner, Montana, told me that his father's most important fly-tying tool during this period was a razor blade. "Hooks were hard to come by during the war," Richard said. "Most were made in Norway, which was blocked by the Nazis, or in England and they were using all their metal to build other things: ships and guns." So Merton tried to tie the flies from Bergman's book on the few hooks he had.

According to Richard, his dad would "tie twelve flies and maybe one of them would look right, so he'd save the one good fly and use the razor blade to cut the other eleven off their hooks and try again." After the war, Merton stockpiled a supply of tying materials and was one of the only local anglers who could tie flies. This attracted a bunch of "friends"

There are many "improved" Sofa Pillow fly patterns, which all descended from Pat Barnes's original creation. But few have been as tested, and proven as effective, as Parks's version. This fly (tied by Richard Parks) is one of my primary options when fish are taking Salmonflies from the surface.

who wanted flies from him, so he began selling them to these guys. Eventually, after a couple family vacations to Yellowstone, the family moved to Montana in 1953, opened Parks' Fly Shop, and the rest is fly-fishing history.

In 1954, Merton developed perhaps Parks' Fly Shop's most recognizable fly pattern and what continues to be their best-selling imitation for the famous Salmonfly (*Pterynarcys* spp.) hatch. Richard says the fly was the first of many Improved Sofa Pillows (an early Salmonfly dry pattern), derived from the original invented by West Yellowstone's Pat Barnes in the 1940s. According to Richard, Merton felt that "the original design was sound enough, but the materials were wrong. Squirrel hair [used as the Sofa Pillow's wing material] doesn't float, and the original fly's body was red!" Most of the Salmonflies that emerge in the park are more of a tangerine-orange color than red. I asked Richard where he sources the perfect orange-colored material that he uses for the Parks' Salmonfly and he said, "I keep my eyes open every time I walk past someone's yarn aisle: Walmart, Joann Fabrics, and other places."

Merton Parks also changed the Sofa Pillow's wing. "Dad used bucktail for the wing and tail. A lot of bucktails have black fibers on the back of them, so I just mix that real good with the brown," Richard said. "Make sure the fly is heavily hackled, and trim the palmered hackle short. It takes a lot of hair stacking to tie this fly. And that's why it takes me ten to twelve minutes to tie one. But it's probably the fly most associated with our fly shop."

Most anglers fish the Parks' Salmonfly as a dry fly, but it also has other uses. Richard says, "It works as well wet as it does dry. Just pull it under [as the fly starts to drag at the end of a drift], and let it run wet." Salmonflies can't swim and a lot of them end up drowned, under the water. This can be a very effective tactic, especially when the hatch is nearing its end and the trout have begun to ignore dry-fly imitations.

Fishing Techniques

Most stoneflies crawl from the water onto dry areas to emerge: boulders and rocks; a fallen tree jutting from beneath the water; grasses, trees, and shrubs along the shore. But know that when the hatch is at its heaviest, enough of the insects, which fly poorly, will land in the middle of rivers and creeks too, so it's worth casting there as well, particularly in low-water years.

Salmonflies often end up struggling on the water's surface after they've inadvertently flown into the current during their search for mates or in an attempt to avoid the many birds and mammals that also want to eat them. Their on-water struggles garner trout attention, and it can be important for anglers to mimic this movement by skittering (intentionally dragging the flies across the water's surface) or twitching the flies by pulling on the fly line.

Near-historic low river flows, combined with an intense Salmonfly emergence, created ideal fishing conditions for the Yellowstone River, inside the park, on this late June morning in 2021. The beautifully colored cuttbow pictured here sipped in my Parks' Salmonfly like it had been waiting for it all spring.

Chubby Chernobyl

The Chubby Chernobyl, often called a "Chubby" by anglers, is by far the most important Yellowstone dry fly for catching trout on the surface as high runoff waters begin to recede during the national park's initial fishing months. The Chubby's history is somewhat murky, though it's known to have descended from the Chernobyl Ant and been altered by a small group of fly tiers and guides along Utah's Green River.

The Chubby is an excellent imitator of the large Salmonflies and Golden Stoneflies that

- **Hook:** #8-14 2XL dry-fly hook or Dai-Riki 730 2XL nymph hook
- **Thread:** 6/0, color to match body
- **Tail:** Krystal Flash, often smolt blue, or color to match body
- **Body:** Usually a synthetic, flashy dubbing, but natural beaver dubbing can also be used to create more-muted patterns. You can use colors to match naturals or more-vivid materials to attract fish.
- **Overbody:** Fly foam (2 mm), often tan, though black and other colors are often used
- **Legs:** Flat latex or rubber legs
- **Wings:** Polypropylene yarn or MFC Widow's Web, most often white

emerge in the park. But it's also a passable grasshopper imitation that will continue to garner trout attention after the fish have turned their appetites from predominantly aquatic-born insects to searching the surface for terrestrials (land-born insects) in the summer. There are some seasons where it's the

There are few stonefly dry imitations more versatile than the Chubby. Anglers can imitate any stonefly species (grasshoppers too) by simply altering the size of the hook and color of the fly's materials. I catch most of my early season dry-fly-eating trout on Chubbies.

only dry-fly pattern I tie to my leader in the park for over a month.

Chubbies work very well as highly visible, buoyant, stand-alone dry flies. They excel at being blind cast (fishing the water where you expect a fish to be, not necessarily where you've already seen one) to in-stream structure: things like submerged trees and vegetation, the edge between shallow water near the bank and a deeper drop-off, and riffles and boulder-strewn runs.

I usually begin the season fishing very large Chubbies, up to a size 8, which is a reasonable girth when you consider the size of the Salmonflies for which the trout often mistake them. But as the days march on, continuing through summer, I begin reducing the size of the Chubbies I fish. I begin by dropping down a size to 10s, getting ever smaller as the season progresses and the water drops, until I'm tying size 14s to my line. Trout have a more difficult time seeing the obvious non-living attributes of a smaller fly pattern, and many of them will have already been caught on giant Chubbies, making them reluctant to repeat that mistake in the lower, clearer waters of late summer.

Fishing Techniques

As effective as Chubbies are at catching trout on their own, they are even better when used as the lead fly in a two-fly tandem rig with a sinking pattern tied to the bend of the Chubby's hook. This turns the Chubby into a de facto strike indicator that gets pulled subsurface when a fish eats the sinking fly beneath it. But it's a strike indicator with a hook that's just as likely to be eaten by a trout. I generally reduce the leader length for my guiding clients when I'm using a Chubby two-fly rig. A 7½-foot 3X or 4X leader, rather than the common 9-foot leader often used when fishing a single dry fly, is just much easier for most people to cast, especially with the potential

for wind, which often appears in the park in the afternoon.

Chubbies are also commonly used as the lead in two-fly dry-fly rigs, where the highly visible Chubby helps you find a much less visible dry fly on the water. I usually tie the less visible fly to the Chubby's hook bend with an 18- to 24-inch piece of tippet. You want the tippet short enough to help you find the less visible fly, yet long enough to create separation between the two so the flies don't end up in a tangled pile on the water. Any smaller, less visible fly pattern can be used as the dropper fly, but I often use darker, more muted patterns that I have trouble seeing when fishing them by themselves.

You can fish this rig either by blind casting it or presenting it to fish that are already rising. Use the Chubby as a guide to find the smaller fly. If you still cannot see it, you at least know approximately where it should be on the water based upon where you see the Chubby floating. If any fish rises near your Chubby, gently lift your rod tip to set the hook.

Chubbies are tied with foam bodies, which make them very buoyant, and their bright white wings are highly visible for anglers. These traits are perfect for use in a dry-dropper tandem with a nymph. If the Chubby hesitates or sinks, you know a fish has taken the nymph suspended below it. But often the fish will choose the Chubby, like this beautiful Yellowstone cutthroat trout.

George's Rubber Legged Brown Stone Nymph

- **Hook:** #8-10 Mustad 79580 3XL nymph hook
- **Thread:** Brown 6/0
- **Tail and legs:** White thin rubber or silicon
- **Abdomen:** Yellow and brown woven Hareline synthetic yarn
- **Thorax:** Gray hare's ear dubbing

George Anderson and his son James own Anderson's Yellowstone Angler Fly Shop and Guide Service on the southern edge of Livingston, Montana. George is originally from the Catskill Mountains region, an upstate New York trout mecca. He moved west to attend college in Colorado and spent his summers working in West Yellowstone. After college, George and his wife moved to Livingston (where James would eventually be born) and George worked for the legendary Dan Bailey's Fly Shop, which is still in operation in downtown Livingston but now owned by Dale Sexton. George left Bailey's and opened his own shop in 1979. The Andersons have been at the forefront of Montana's and Yellowstone National Park's fly-fishing industry ever since.

When I asked George and James Anderson for one of their favorite Yellowstone flies, James said that George's Rubber Legged Brown Stone, designed by his father, is a good one. The fly (like another pattern, the Amy's Ant, discussed later in this book) achieved fame at the Jackson Hole One Fly event. George won

Woven-bodied nymph patterns, like George's Rubber Legged Brown Stone Nymph, are very popular with some anglers, though you find few of them for sale in fly shops (Anderson's Yellowstone Angler has them) because of the time and effort it takes to tie one. But the flies remain effective, and their woven bodies present the fish with an imitative feature that they don't often see.

the tournament, while setting records for the number of fish he caught, by using his Rubber Legged Brown Stone in 1989 and 1990, the only two years he fished in the competition.

The Rubber Legged Brown Stone has undergone several changes over the years. James told me in an email that "originally there were no rubber legs on his brown stone (or cone heads or bead heads). In later years he added the legs for movement and beads or cones for extra weight to fish the deepest holes." According to James, you can also add "7-8 wraps of round lead-free wire .025 (or just the tungsten cone). That way if you happen to bust off, there is no lead at all in the fly."

George initially used rubber bands to form the legs on his fly. When I was discussing the pattern with him at his shop, he pulled out an old, dusty wooden box that contained some early versions of the fly to quickly illustrate why he moved on from rubber bands: All of the legs made from them had disintegrated over the years.

I asked George and James why they think the pattern is so effective, and why they bother to tie complicated woven fly patterns. George told me, "Years ago, Dan Bailey tied woven bodies, so I did it too." James added, "Woven [bodies] gives you the look of a dark back and light underbelly, just like natural stoneflies. All dubbed [bodies] is still good, but using both techniques is better."

Using the proper yarn to form the fly's body is important. When I asked James where tiers can acquire the proper material to tie the fly, he replied that you need "a synthetic yarn for sure. The original yarn was more coarse and cannot be found anymore. I think you'd almost have better luck buying it from a yarn/sewing shop or Joann Fabrics. Brown and light tan, almost a carpet yarn that looks buggy on a hook."

Fishing Techniques

The Andersons told me that the fly works best in the park during the springtime in the Yellowstone River when the Golden Stones are hatching. But they also fish it for lake-run brown trout on the Madison in the fall. According to James, it works best "fished solo or as the lead fly to help bring a lighter, smaller fly down deep behind it."

Most Golden Stoneflies have a multiyear life cycle, so they are always present in the bottoms of the park rivers and creeks where they live. And nearly all of the park's moving waters (not lakes or ponds) have Golden Stones. I generally fish these types of flies with a 9-foot leader, tapered down to a 3X or 4X tippet, beneath an indicator. Golden Stonefly nymphs don't swim; they generally curl up at their waist when they become dislodged from beneath the submerged rocks. This makes it important to fish the flies, most of the time, on a dead drift, the same speed as the current, near the stream bottom.

This swift-moving water, flowing over and around rocks and boulders, is perfect habitat for Heidi Kosmer and Ruthann Weamer to fish Golden Stonefly imitations like George's Brown Stone.

Jacklin's Golden Stone

- **Hook:** #6-8 Dai-Riki 700
- **Thread:** Rusty brown 6/0
- **Tail (egg sac):** Clipped deer hair, dyed brown
- **Rib:** Ginger clipped hackle
- **Body:** Golden Stonefly natural dubbing
- **Wing:** Blond elk hair, tied in at a 45-degree angle
- **Legs:** Brown round rubber (small)
- **Head and collar:** Tan elk hair, tied bullet style

As snowmelt runoff begins to subside in Yellowstone National Park, Salmonflies generally begin to emerge. These large stoneflies get the trout looking towards the surface, and their often prolific numbers create a natural wonder that every fly fisher should witness at least once in their lifetime. But there's another big stonefly that you'll often find intermixed with these supersized black and orange insects: Golden Stoneflies. These slightly smaller stoneflies are still large creatures, but they look a little different than the Salmonflies.

Golden Stones (most species are in the Perlidae family) generally have lighter wings than Salmonflies. Their bodies are often yellow, gold, or even shades of olive. The term "Golden Stonefly" is just a common name—a name given by anglers to stoneflies that look and act similar, at least in the ways that matter to fly fishing. But these common names don't really consider specific entomological differences that define families and species for scientific purposes. This causes some other stoneflies, like the Nocturnal Stones, which

Salmonflies get all the glory, but imitating Golden Stoneflies can be just as productive when they appear. This Jacklin's Golden Stone (tied by Bob Jacklin) is very similar to Mr. Jacklin's Salmonfly, differing only by hook size and material color. It's a great searching pattern for use when you're prospecting with a dry fly early in the season.

can appear in the park in late summer, to also be called "Golden Stones" by some anglers. But the Nocturnal Stones, with their flightless males, are very different creatures from a biological standpoint. Luckily for us anglers, the fish don't necessarily differentiate stonefly species either. They eat all of them.

Because most Golden Stoneflies look and behave in a similar fashion to Salmonflies, anglers often imitate them by using smaller hooks to tie smaller patterns that are often tied exactly the same as Salmonflies, but differently colored. That's what Bob Jacklin, the West Yellowstone fly-fishing icon and owner of Jacklin's Fly Shop, has done with his Golden Stone. Mr. Jacklin's Giant Salmonfly dry is one of the best fly patterns for imitating those stoneflies in the park (and elsewhere). And his Golden Stone, with its clipped deer hair egg sac, is just as effective.

Jacklin's pattern can be used to imitate newly emerged Golden Stonefly adults, but because he includes a trimmed deer hair tail, shaped to look like an egg sac, it is a great choice when you're trying to imitate females as they're dropping their eggs into the water. It's not always necessary, from a trout-catching standpoint, to imitate egg sacs, but it doesn't hurt either. I don't believe I've ever had a trout refuse my stonefly dry because it had an egg sac when the fish were eating recently hatched adults or males that do not carry eggs.

Fishing Techniques

Golden Stoneflies, just like most stonefly species, crawl from the water as nymphs to emerge on streamside vegetation or rocks. So you should target these areas when you are blind casting Jacklin's Golden Stone. Make sure to use floatant on the flies, as the pattern's hollow-hair design will quickly absorb water and sink if you do not. Some anglers intentionally slap their big stonefly patterns

to the water's surface to induce a predatory strike from the fish, and this does work well at times. But you have to do it with a little finesse: I've had guiding clients slam stonefly dries like Jacklin's so hard to the water that the force unintentionally submerges the pattern. Aim your cast just a few inches above the water, rather than directly into it, and the fly will still plop a little onto the surface.

The park's trout are beginning to get a little more wary as the Golden Stoneflies make their appearance. Some of them will have been caught on very similar-looking Salmonfly dries and will be hesitant to make that mistake again. Adding a little movement to your Golden Stone by twitching or gently skittering it across the surface can help catch trout that want to make sure this big bug is alive before they eat it. I fish these large stonefly dries with a 9-foot leader and 3X or 4X tippet. If you use tippet that's too light, the prominent deer hair wing on Jacklin's Golden Stone (and other similar, large patterns) will spin and get twisted by the air as you cast, and your leader will end in a tangled mess.

The vast majority of stoneflies crawl to dry ground to emerge into adults outside the water, like this Pteronarcys *nymph has done. This means that they have to fall or fly onto the surface for trout to have the opportunity to eat them.*

- **Hook:** #12-16 competition hook or jig hook, such as the Daiichi 4647, or standard heavy nymph hook
- **Thread:** Tan 6/0
- **Bead:** Black
- **Abdomen:** Bright green latex
- **Thorax:** Hare's ear dubbing with guard hairs

Czech Caddis

Competitive fly fishers, whose numbers have grown in recent years, have provided Yellowstone National Park's anglers with several effective fly patterns. Most store-supplied nymphs contain barbed hooks that have to be mashed down to make them legal. But these days, you have the option to purchase barbless hooks, and the flies tied on them, that are often designed for use in competitive fly-fishing tournaments. Most fly-fishing competitions, and Yellowstone National Park, share some of the same rules, and one of them is barbless hooks.

Competition rules also state that no weight is allowed to be added to your leader. But you can use split shot in Yellowstone, as long as it's not made from lead. However, this competition rule has led to the creation of new, heavier nymph patterns, designed to sink quickly due to body shape (such as the Perdigon) and/or the incorporation of heavy beads, sometimes in conjunction with a fly-sized jig hook, like the Czech Caddis. The quick-sinking nature of these flies makes adding additional weight to your leader often unnecessary. And that's

The Czech Caddis sinks quickly and is less likely to snag the stream bottom due to the manner in which its jig hook suspends the fly from an angler's leader. The flies look like caddis larvae, which hatch throughout the season, keeping them on trout menus.

a good thing. I despise split shot because it often gets caught in stream-bottom rocks and debris and causes you to break off your flies as you attempt to free them, or the split shot begins to slide down your leader as you cast, stopping at your fly and forcing you to move it back to its original position. Split shot remains an important tool, at times, when you're fishing particularly deep stretches of swift-moving water. But if I can catch fish without using it, I'll gladly choose that option.

Caddis larvae, which the Czech Caddis imitates, look like little worms and some (but not all) of their bodies are olive to bright green in color. The larvae of the famed *Brachycentrus* species caddis, known as the Mother's Day Caddis in the West and the Grannom in the East, are a bright green color, though they can begin hatching in some park waters before they're open to fishing, or sometimes when the water is too high for good fishing. But that doesn't mean the fish won't still eat flies that look like them throughout the rest of the season. And there are other caddis larvae species with green or olive bodies that will be found when the park's waters are open and conditions have improved.

Many trout are caught throughout the park on caddis larvae imitations, and anytime the fish are ignoring your nymphs, it's a good idea to try one. Who knows, maybe you'll even catch the largest fish of your life. Bob Jacklin, the famed West Yellowstone fly angler, caught his "Fish of a Lifetime," a 30-inch, 10-pound leviathan brown trout, in the Madison River (outside the park) in 2006. It took a caddis nymph that looked very similar to the Czech Caddis.

Fishing Techniques

I prefer to fish size 14 Czech Caddis with a 9-foot leader and 4X tippet, dropped off the bend of the hook from a larger, heavier fly, such as a size 12 Perdigon, to help it sink quickly into the trout feeding zone. I generally fish both flies beneath a highly visible, buoyant indicator such as a brightly colored Thingamabobber. It's generally best to fish caddis larvae patterns the same speed as the current, though stripping the flies back to you at the end of the drift will occasionally produce fish.

The Czech Caddis pictured here is tied with a bright green body, and that's my favorite version. But caddis larvae can also range in color from olive to shades of tan and brown to yellow and orange. On any given day, a Czech Caddis tied in any of these colors could be the better fly.

Make sure to use heavy enough leaders and tippet (3X or 4X) so that you're able to retrieve your flies most of the time when they get stuck on the stream bottom. And they should get stuck every once in a while or you're probably not getting them deep enough. Try adjusting the distance from your strike indicator to your flies or add weight to help the flies sink deeper in the water column.

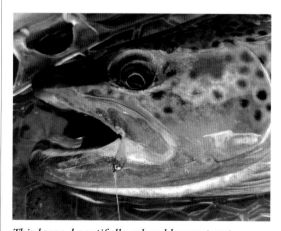

This large, beautifully colored brown trout, caught on a Czech Caddis in the park, was not close to the size of Bob Jacklin's "Fish of a Lifetime," but both of those trout ate flies that look very similar. The Czech Caddis works well throughout the entirety of the park's fishing season.

X Caddis

- **Hook:** #12-22 standard dry-fly hook
- **Thread:** 8/0, color to match dubbed body
- **Shuck:** Caddis gold, green, or tan (depending upon the specific pupal shuck the tier is imitating) Zelon
- **Body:** Antron, Zelon, or natural dubbing (I prefer beaver dubbing for natural). Tan, olive, green, amber, brown, and black are the most popular colors.
- **Wing:** Stacked natural deer hair

If I had to choose one caddis dry-fly imitation to carry in my fly boxes, it would be, without a doubt, an X Caddis. The X Caddis was invented by West Yellowstone fly-fishing legends Craig Mathews and John Juracek, though that information doesn't tell the pattern's whole story. You can find the rest of the X Caddis's history on Mr. Mathews's website (craigmathewsyellowstone.com), where he states, "While John [Juracek] and I developed the X Caddis to fool the large resident rainbow trout of the Henry's Fork, it was my wife Jackie

who came up with the idea of incorporating the flies['] trailing-shimmering, sparkling shuck." Mathews continues, "Her reasoning was simple . . . If super selective trout took our world-famous Sparkle Duns with their trailing shuck for emerging and crippled-impaired mayflies[,] why wouldn't the same thing work with the caddis imitations too?"

Caddisflies belong to a very important family of aquatic insects that are vital to imitate if you want to consistently catch trout in Yellowstone National Park. Emerging caddis ride gas

Craig Mathews and John Juracek's X Caddis is one of the most effective caddis dry-fly imitations in the world. But perhaps the fly should have been named "Jackie's Caddis," since it was Mr. Mathews's wife's idea to add the trailing shuck that transformed the pattern into something special.

bubbles, emanating from inside their pupal shuck, to reach the surface. This often gets the fish excited and they chase these fast-moving flies, sometimes overpowering their attack and breaking through the water's surface.

Very buoyant caddis patterns like the Elk Hair Caddis, and its foam-tied versions, are often fished in riffled water. But you will sometimes find trout feeding on spent caddis (dying female insects that have laid their eggs and are lying motionless on the water) or even caddis species emerging on flatter river sections—glides below a riffle and calm pools. These fish may be a little less eager to accept a high-floating, heavily hackled fly. And that's where the X Caddis shines.

The X Caddis's trailing Zelon shuck imitates the remnants of the pupal body, which is still attached as the fly becomes an adult. Even though the shuck is no longer present in spent caddis—they have previously shed this skin, mated, and have died or are in the process of doing so—the trout will often ignore the shuck and eat the X Caddis because it lies flush on the water's surface. But if you find trout that are particularly picky, you can always take your nippers and cut off all, or most, of the X Caddis's shuck to make it a near-perfect match for the spent caddis.

Fishing Techniques

Bucky McCormick, the manager of Craig Mathews's former West Yellowstone fly shop, Blue Ribbon Flies (he sold it several years ago), was a tremendous help as I wrote this book. Bucky emailed me some of the fly shop's information about the X Caddis, which stated, "We fish the fly as a dry, and dress it with floatant. Upstream, dead drift, is the most productive method, casting to individual fish if they are rising. As with mayflies, caddis can experience difficulties emerging from their pupal shucks at times. Many end up trapped in their shucks entirely, or with the shuck trailing off their bodies, and with wings fully emerged."

Trout look for easy meals so they can get the highest return while burning calories to feed. Any aquatic insect that is incapable of flight because it's still attached to its shuck creates the type of food source that fish want.

If you find trout making bulging rises, where their backs and not their mouths penetrate the surface as they feed on a caddis hatch, the fish are probably eating caddis emergers just below the surface. You can use an X Caddis here too. Cast a little farther ahead (about 2 feet) and just beyond the fish you're targeting, and pull on your fly line (so the fly is pulled back into the fish's feeding lane) to make the X Caddis sink. As the fly approaches a bulging fish, add a little slack to your leader by wiggling your rod to release some fly line. This eases your line tension, allowing the X Caddis to reappear on the surface like an emerging insect.

*Caddisflies appear in many different colors and sizes throughout the season. This Mother's Day Caddis (*Brachycentrus spp.*) is a member of one of the most angler-anticipated emergences of the year.*

Elk Hair Caddis

- **Hook:** #10-20 standard dry-fly hook
- **Thread:** 8/0, color to match dubbed body
- **Body:** Thread, dubbing, floss, peacock herl (pictured here), or synthetic material
- **Rib (optional):** Copper, silver, or gold wire (fine)
- **Hackle:** Brown, palmered along the body
- **Wing:** Elk or deer body hair, stacked to align tips

The Elk Hair Caddis was created by Pennsylvania-born fly fisherman Al Troth in the 1950s, but it didn't achieve world-wide acclaim until Mr. Troth moved to Montana and began guiding fly fishers in the early 1970s. Troth's signature fly pattern (he invented others as well) began to circulate by word of mouth before it was featured in a 1978 edition of *Fly Tyer* magazine. Since then, the Elk Hair Caddis has become arguably the most commonly fished dry-fly caddis imitation in the world.

One of the Elk Hair Caddis's greatest design features is its adaptability. Caddisflies in Yellowstone National Park appear in a wide array of colors each season, and they are present for nearly the entire fishing season. Fly tiers can imitate every caddis hatch with an Elk Hair Caddis by simply changing the color of the pattern's materials and the size of the hook used to tie them. My favorite size Elk Hair Caddis for the park is a size 12 or 14, often tied with shades of brown, tan, or green bodies. But you'll also want to have some white

Al Troth's Elk Hair Caddis is one of the best-known fly patterns in the world. It is often one of the first flies new tiers learn to tie. Elk Hair Caddises float very well and are an excellent choice to catch fish eating caddis adults in any of the park's more turbulent rivers and creeks.

ones if you plan to fish the Firehole's famed *Nectopsyche* hatch, known to anglers as the "White Miller."

The Firehole's White Miller hatch may be the most famous caddis emergence in the park, but in a strange twist, it's one of the rarest. The hatch also appears in limited numbers on the Gibbon and Madison; how important it is to catching trout on these rivers is a matter of opinion. But if you're fishing the Firehole River when the park opens, later in the summer, or before it closes for the season, you should have a pattern to imitate the White Miller.

One of the marks of a great fly pattern is the way in which it's adapted over the years. Mr. Troth created variations of his fly to imitate crickets and grasshoppers, but two of my favorite Elk Hair Caddis adaptations are Hans Weilenmann's CDC & Elk and the Foam Caddis. The CDC & Elk uses a cul de canard (CDC) feather tied beneath the fly's elk hair wing, instead of a rooster hackle, to instill lifelike movement and represent legs. I use the CDC & Elk anywhere I'd use the original Elk Hair Caddis, but it excels in flatter-water applications in and around pools, where the fish may want the fly to sit more flush to the water's surface. The Foam Caddis is tied exactly like the Elk Hair Caddis, but a thin foam sheet is shaped to form the body, wing, and/or head. This makes a terrifically buoyant pattern float even better.

The Orvis website includes a remembrance of Al Troth, written by Phil Monahan in August 2012. It also features a video interview by Sporting Fly, featuring Mr. Troth and his son, Eric. You can find the video at news.orvis.com/fly-fishing/Remembering-Al-Troth.

Fishing Techniques

You can fish the Elk Hair Caddis, and its various adaptations, either to imitate a specific hatch being eaten by a rising fish or as a searching pattern when you're blind casting. Like nearly all my dry flies, I begin presenting my Elk Hair Caddis without movement on a dead drift. But because the fly floats so well, it's an excellent option for skittering (intentionally dragging) across the water to make it appear alive.

You can also adapt your Elk Hair Caddis streamside to try to imitate insects behaving in specific ways. If most of the trout are eating caddis in flat pools, and they're showing hesitation to your high-floating dry fly, you can take your nippers and trim the hackle flush on the fly's underside to help it sit lower on the water. You can also shorten the wing by trimming it so the fly hangs by its head, appearing more like an emerging caddis.

The Elk Hair Caddis's foam variation floats longer without the need for re-dressing it as often with floatant. Though I believe you lose some of the Elk Hair Caddis's realism when you replace it with the foam version, this matters most often when fishing flat water. I prefer the Foam Caddis as a dropper, used in tandem with a larger foam fly such as a Chubby. A fish will occasionally accept the smaller Foam Caddis when it's intrigued by, but rejects, the larger Chubby. The foam version also floats a little better if you're using it as the lead dry fly in a dropper rig with a nymph. But these flies are generally small, so make sure you use a size-appropriate nymph, such as a size 12 or 14 Perdigon, to reduce the chances your dry fly will be submerged by the nymph's weight.

Goddard Caddis

- **Hook:** #10-16 standard dry-fly hook
- **Thread:** Tan 6/0
- **Body/wing:** Spun deer or elk body hair, trimmed into shape of a caddis wing
- **Hackle:** Brown
- **Antennae:** Hackle stems or synthetic Microfibbets (similar to paintbrush fibers)

My friend John Campbell, originally from upstate New York, now lives in Gallatin Gateway, just outside of the ultra-trendy, high-priced Big Sky, Montana, community. John's cabin is relatively close (Montana-close) to the West Entrance at West Yellowstone, giving him ample opportunities to fish in the park.

John fondly recalls his first fishing trip to Yellowstone National Park in 1997 with his mother, when he was still learning to fly fish and didn't really know what to do with so much water at his disposal. He was perusing the items for sale at the park store in Roosevelt when an elderly man asked him where he was headed. John told him that he wanted to fish, but really didn't have a plan. "I could have caught trout out my truck window this morning," the old man said. "Go to Yellowstone Lake, between eight and ten in the morning, and fish one of these." The man gave John a fly. "You'll see fish sipping bugs from the surface, cruising around looking for more. Cast this fly a foot or two in front of them, and they'll eat it just as it begins sink."

The Goddard Caddis was originally designed in England as a lake fly, but the pattern works equally well in the park's rivers and creeks. It sits flush to the water's surface, making it a little more difficult for anglers to see, but remains very buoyant because it's tied from only elk hair and hackle.

John took the fly and followed the man's directions. When he arrived at Fishing Bridge, he could see trout surface-feeding, down the lakeshore, just inside his casting range. The first fish he cast to ate the fly just like the old man said it would. John landed a 21-inch Yellowstone cutthroat and then continued to land four more similar-sized fish before the remaining trout moved to deeper water as the sun rose high in the sky. John was ecstatic, and as he headed back to his car he clipped the fly from his leader so he wouldn't lose it and to make sure he got more of them. It was a Goddard Caddis.

The Goddard Caddis was originally named the G&H Sedge when it was designed as a lake fly in England by John Goddard and Clive Henry. It's a fly pattern that's been used to catch trout for a long time. Made from mostly (or entirely) natural materials, it's one of those flies that has fallen from angler favor through no fault of its own. But that's a great benefit for those who continue to fish the Goddard Caddis. The park's trout see fewer of them these days, and that helps to keep the fish from becoming callous to it.

Yellowstone Lake's fishing and fishing regulations aren't the same as when John first fished it in the mid-'90s. Nonnative lake trout entered the lake and overwhelmed the native cutthroat population. But through a monumental restoration effort to curtail lake trout populations by netting them and destroying their eggs, the lake's native fish are rebounding, and there is hope on the horizon.

Fishing Techniques

The Goddard Caddis's air-trapping, spun-hair body and wing make this fly very buoyant, particularly when it is dressed with floatant before it gets wet, and it works as well in rivers and creeks as it does in lakes. But the fly sits flush on the water, making it more difficult to see than the Elk Hair or Foam Caddis,

John Campbell wades into one of his favorite park waters, hoping a trout will rise for his Goddard Caddis. The water in front of John is braided, moving, but without cascading white water that would make a flush-floating fly like the Goddard Caddis difficult to see.

which can also be tied with brightly colored overwings to increase their visibility. If you're having difficulty tracking the fly on the water, it's a good idea to fish it as a dropper, tied to the bend of the hook, from a more visible fly such as a Chubby.

The ability to spin deer hair to tie the fly—where you take a clump of deer body hair and use your tying thread to spin it evenly around the hook, then trim it to shape—is generally considered to be one of the more advanced fly-tying techniques. The key is to stop yourself from using too large a clump of hair, trying to create the whole body in one shot, instead of using several smaller clumps. Hold the hair above the hook, make a loose thread wrap around it, then pull it tight to the hook shank with a second wrap while allowing the hair to spin around the shank.

After the body has been spun, you need to trim it into shape. Some tiers use razor blades, which helps them form the fly quickly (after they do it enough times to get good at it), but you can also shape the fly with your tying scissors. Don't cut off too much hair at once. You can always cut a second time, but you can never reattach the hair you've trimmed.

Coachman Trude

- **Hook:** #10-16 2XL standard dry-fly hook
- **Thread:** Black 8/0
- **Tail:** Fibers from a golden pheasant crest
- **Body:** Peacock herl
- **Wing:** White calf tail
- **Hackle:** Coachman brown

When I asked Richard Parks, the legendary owner of Parks' Fly Shop in Gardiner, Montana, which sits so close to Yellowstone's North Entrance that you can almost see the famed Gateway Arch from its stoop, to name his favorite Yellowstone National Park fly pattern, he replied, "A size 12 Coachman Trude with a Prince Nymph dropped off it has caught a lot of fish." His answer may surprise a lot of Yellowstone's younger fly fishers, but he would know much better than most. There may be no other angler who has more knowledge of Yellowstone's trout, and the places in which they live, than Mr. Parks.

The Coachman Trude is an old-school fly pattern—created and popularized in the early 1900s—that has fallen from favor with many of today's anglers who'd rather toss more modern, high-floating foam flies. "Trude" is a dry-fly style, defined by the incorporation of a wing formed with a single clump of hair (most often calf tail), tied swept back over the body; a tail most often made from feather fibers (usually golden pheasant crest); a peacock

This Coachman Trude (tied by Richard Parks) is one of the oldest fly patterns in this book. But because we fly anglers often seek the newest fly designs, older flies are sometimes neglected, and that can increase their effectiveness. The Coachman Trude has been catching trout in the park for a long time, and it'll catch them this season too.

herl or fur-dubbed body; and several turns of dry-fly hackle near the fly's head.

It's the exact combination of materials a tier uses that delineates one Trude from another. For instance, the Coachman Trude pictured here would become a Royal Coachman Trude if the tier (Richard Parks) had decided to form a band of red thread or floss in the middle of the fly's peacock herl body. Changes to the materials, or their colors, from one Trude to the next are an attempt to achieve a desired effect, such as imitating the body color of a specific insect or simply trying to provoke a trout to strike by the incorporation of red thread.

As we stood discussing Parks's fondness for the Coachman Trude, he turned around and looked through an old wooden cabinet behind his counter and produced two that he had tied. He handed the flies to me as he began to speak about the peacock herl used to form the pattern's body. "There's something magic about peacock. It just worms its way into a fish's beady little brain, and they turn it into whatever they want it to be," he said. Peacock herl's shimmering, green iridescence

Yellowstone icon Richard Parks at the counter of his fly shop in Gardiner, Montana, just outside the park's North Entrance. There are very few anglers who know the park's trout waters as well as Mr. Parks.

gives the appearance of movement—life—as it reflects light. And anytime a material like that is added to a fly pattern, it often results in something trout want to eat.

But Coachman Trudes have other great fish-catching qualities. "It's a double threat, that you can fish wet or dry," Parks told me. "And it's visible—the fish are not alarmed by a white thing floating down the river," a reference to the pattern's prominent, white calf-tail hair wing, which allows anglers to find the fly on the water more easily. Any fly pattern that's still catching fish a hundred years after its creation is one you should probably have in your box. The Coachman Trude's versatility is its best attribute and the reason why you should try one in Yellowstone this year.

Fishing Techniques

As Mr. Parks stated, the Coachman Trude can be fished wet or dry.

If you want to fish the Coachman Trude solely as a dry fly, make sure to use floatant to help repel water, which its natural materials will quickly absorb if left untreated. If you want to fish the fly as a wet, squeeze water into it after you tie it to your leader to help it sink more quickly. Cast across the water and mend your fly line to allow the fly to sink. As it is floating past you, hold your line tight to cause the fly to drag, rising from the stream bottom and appearing like an emerging insect. You can also fish a Trude like a streamer, to imitate a baitfish, by stripping it back to you with short, quick pulls on your fly line.

Some anglers like to fish the Coachman Trude as both a dry and a wet in the same cast. To do this, fish the fly on the surface until it begins to drag. Then tug on your line to cause the fly to sink. Now strip it back to you with short, quick tugs on your line. False cast the fly several times to help it shed water, and it will now briefly float again for the next cast.

Rubberleg Stimulator

- **Hook:** #8-16 Daichi 1260 or any curved stonefly hook
- **Thread:** 8/0, color to match body
- **Tail:** Stacked elk or deer hair
- **Rib (optional):** Copper or gold wire (fine)
- **Legs:** Round rubber (small)
- **Palmered body hackle:** Brown
- **Wing:** Stacked elk or deer hair
- **Head hackle:** Grizzly
- **Head:** Flashy synthetic dubbing, often a contrasting color to what you've used for the body

The Stimulator, often affectionately known by anglers as a "Stimie," has an interesting origin. Two well-known fly tiers, Randall Kaufmann and Jim Slattery, are both often mentioned as the pattern's creator. This happens more than you may realize. There are a lot of fly tiers around the world trying to match similar hatches, to catch similar-behaving trout, with mostly the same fly-tying materials.

I've been told that Jim Slattery tied and named the first Stimulator, while Randall Kaufmann refined the fly, giving us the Stimulator that most anglers now fish. But I don't know whether that's true. And if you really want to get picky, the Stimulator is very similar in form to the Sofa Pillow, which was tied even earlier, in the mid-twentieth century, by West Yellowstone's legendary Pat Barnes. This murkiness may seem odd now that we have computers and social media, which seem to broadcast every fly tier's new pet project almost immediately after it falls from their vise. But in the days dominated by slow media—books and magazines—fly patterns tended to

Adding rubber legs to a Stimulator gives a modern twist to a fly that's been in use for a long time. Stimulators are good imitations for stoneflies, but they're also highly effective as a general searching pattern when trout aren't visibly rising to a hatch.

be more localized in nature until they were published and the literature reached a wide audience. By then, the pattern may have been reinvented or copied and transformed many times over by other tiers who also feel their changes "created" the fly.

Thankfully, trout don't really care who created any of our flies. They just know whether they want to eat them or not. And lots of trout like to eat Stimulators. As I mentioned, this fly style looks quite similar to the Sofa Pillow, but Stimulators are tied with more-buoyant materials and often in much smaller sizes (the Sofa Pillow was intended to mimic large stoneflies), which make it much more versatile.

If you tie a Stimulator in size 14 or 16, depending upon the color of materials you choose, the fly can be a very good imitation of little stoneflies like the Yellow Sally. Or it can be taken for a larger caddis or even a caterpillar. Keep the pattern larger (size 8 or 10), and tied with an orange or yellow body, and it's an excellent (though more buoyant) Salmonfly or Golden Stonefly imitation. Add rubber legs, and it begins to look more like a grasshopper. I generally prefer to add the rubber legs to my Stimulators—after all, every insect has legs, right? Well maybe not caterpillars, but you get the point. And the fine, small rubber legs can sometimes shudder on the water if there's a breeze, which makes the pattern appear alive.

Fishing Techniques

How you fish your Stimulator really depends upon what you're trying to mimic. If you want it to be taken for a grasshopper, cast it towards drop-offs in the streambed where shallow meets deeper water, flowing adjacent to grassy banks. Twitching the fly by pulling on your line to gently move it can instigate a trout to rise; hoppers don't want to be in the water, and they tend to struggle to get out when they find themselves there.

For imitating caddis or stoneflies, I tend to fish the Stimulator drag-free without intentionally moving it. Often when I'm fishing this way, I'm blind casting, searching for a trout that's looking for a meal. You can skate (drag the fly along the surface by holding or pulling on your line) and twitch the fly here too, because adult caddis and stoneflies, unless they have just laid their eggs and are dying, are also trying to get out of the water. But if you fish the fly with imparted movement, just make sure you're using heavy tippet (no smaller than 3X), because if a trout grabs it, most often the strike is violent, which leads to break-offs if you are using lighter tippet. Trout are imperfect creatures like us. So if you're skating the fly, they will sometimes miss as they attempt to grab it. I find that a miss will make the fish less likely to eat your fly on your next cast. Wild trout don't live long by wasting calories.

Blind casting a Rubberleg Stimulator brought this beautiful brown trout to Ruthann Weamer's net on a slow day in the park. Sometimes it's fun to fish dry flies simply because you want to do it, even when there isn't a hatch occurring. You never know what might decide to eat your fly.

Chubby Sally

- **Hook:** #14 2XL dry-fly hook
- **Thread:** Yellow 6/0
- **Tail:** Red hackle fibers, hair, or synthetic yarn
- **Body:** Bright yellow natural or synthetic dubbing
- **Legs:** Yellow Barred Sili Legs
- **Overbody:** Yellow fly foam (2 mm)
- **Wings:** White polypropylene yarn or MFC Widow's Web

Yellow Sally adults are often small, bright yellow stoneflies, though their color varies from pale yellow to orange (most often females carrying eggs) to greenish. They belong to the genera *Isoperla, Chloroperlidae, Sweltsa,* and *Alloperla,* among others. I've grouped these insects together with the same common name, even though they belong to several different genera (instead of just one like most aquatic insects), because fly anglers often refer to any small, brightly colored yellow stonefly as a Yellow Sally. And they often call small, green ones Green or Olive Sallies. Common names given to aquatic insects are used without a scientific basis—it's just what fly fishers call insects for fishing purposes. This can sometimes cause confusion if you're trying to discuss an exact species, but for the purposes of this book, I'll stick with the common name, Yellow Sally (or the plural, Sallies).

Yellow Sallies are much smaller than the springtime Salmonflies and Golden Stoneflies. They are generally about a size 14, though even smaller ones are also common. Many of

The Chubby Sally is just a variation of the standard Chubby, discussed earlier in the book. But this variation is highly effective due to its smaller size (generally a size 14) and the importance of Yellow Sally hatches in park waters.

the eastern United States' trout fisheries also have populations of these beautiful aquatic insects, though I've never found them to be as important there as they are in western trout streams, including those found in Yellowstone National Park. The best places to find trout eating Yellow Sallies in the East are usually somewhat sterile brook trout streams where the fish have limited options for food. But in the West, they often appear in very heavy numbers, and though they remain an important food source in most of the park's smaller backcountry trout streams, they can be just as important in the large, primary rivers flowing along valley floors.

My favorite fly pattern to imitate this hatch is a Chubby variation specifically designed to imitate the Yellow Sally. When Chubbies initially took the fly-fishing world by storm, they were large patterns, designed to imitate the biggest stoneflies and hoppers. But over time, tiers began to realize the importance of creating smaller Chubbies, size 14 and under. It was from this influx of diminutive Chubbies that the Chubby Sally emerged.

Chubby Sallies can be used anytime as attractor dry flies, which means they'll sometimes work even if you're not seeing naturals on the water. While it's common to see heavy Yellow Sally emergences a couple times each season, it's just as common to see a few of the flies emerging during hatches of other aquatic insects, so the trout see enough of them, for a long enough period, that they'll often eat one even if there are only a few on the water.

Fishing Tactics

I usually expect to begin fishing my Chubby Sallies sometime after the big stoneflies have ended, though there is some overlap, and it's common to find these little stoneflies on the water at the same time as the big, premier stonefly hatches. In a small backcountry stream, I generally use a 7 ½-foot 4X leader. But in the larger rivers, I extend that leader to 9 feet for fishing in the flatter pools.

Most of the time, I fish a Chubby Sally by itself and just prospect (blind cast) for trout that are looking to eat dry flies. Chubby Sallies float very well, and in spite of their reduced size, they remain visible even when blind casting them around in-stream boulders within turbulent riffles and runs. Their buoyancy allows them to suspend a nymph if you choose to fish the flies in a tandem rig. I will also sometimes fish a Chubby Sally behind a larger Chubby, as the dropper fly, or as the primary dry in a terrestrial tandem rig with a floating or sinking ant or beetle.

Note: The red hackle fibers on the Chubby Sally's tail is thought to imitate the natural's egg sac, which is often colored blood-orange. Tiers add this red or orange tail to many different Yellow Sally dry-fly patterns. But it may also just be a triggering mechanism, colorful enough to get the trout's attention and giving them a reason to eat the fly.

This Gardner River brown trout was hiding beside a boulder in a riffle. It rose to take a Chubby Sally on its first drift through the run. Trout sometimes search out smaller, less threatening fly patterns like the Chubby Sally after they have been hooked by larger Chubbies earlier in the season.

Harrop's Green Drake Hair Wing

- **Hook:** #10-14 standard dry-fly hook (#12 is my preferred size for these flies)
- **Thread:** Black 8/0
- **Tail:** Moose mane, divided into two clumps
- **Body:** Olive dubbing
- **Rib:** Yellow heavy thread
- **Hackle:** Grizzly, dyed olive, trimmed flush on the bottom
- **Wing:** Stacked elk or deer hair fibers

René Harrop is one of the world's most innovative and revered fly designers. His patterns have been proven on some of America's most technical dry-fly rivers, like Mr. Harrop's home water, Idaho's Henry's Fork. The Henry's Fork is a dry-fly paradise composed of large flat pools, prolific aquatic insect hatches, and high-pressured, discerning trout that generally won't eat just any fly you throw at them. It can test your angling abilities as well as your fly pattern selection. So when I use Harrop's flies for fishing to the generally much-less-picky Yellowstone National Park trout, it sometimes feels like he has given me an unfair advantage.

The Green Drake Hair Wing might be my favorite Harrop fly pattern. Western Green Drakes are one of the park's premier mayfly hatches because the bugs are large, the fish love to eat them, and the various types of mayflies we anglers loosely call "Western Green Drakes"—including the Lesser Green Drake, Drake Mackerel, Flav, and Great Red Quill, aka Hecuba—can be found hatching

René Harrop's Green Drake Hair Wing is one of the best patterns for imitating emerging mayflies in the park. Even if the fish are obviously eating fully formed adults on the surface, I seldom have them reject this fly.

throughout much of the season. Except for the Hecubas, these flies are all from the genus *Drunella*, which means they are very similar mayflies, hatching and completing their life cycles in comparable fashion. But even the Great Red Quill (Hecuba) mayflies, which are members of the genus *Timpanoga*, look and behave very similarly to the *Drunella* species of Western Green Drakes.

These Green Drakes (they're all "Western" when compared to the completely unrelated "Eastern" Green Drake) often labor as they transition from nymphs to duns in the water's surface film. They twitch, sometimes get stuck in their nymphal shuck, and can generally take a longer period of time than other mayfly species to obtain flight. Once they do, they often flutter and hop on the water as they initially test their wings. Trout find all of this behavior, encompassed in such a large, calorie-filled package, to be irresistible.

This Harrop emerger works well for a couple reasons. First, though the fly is designed to lie flush on the water's surface, resembling a Green Drake emerger that is having trouble extricating itself from its nymphal shuck, it remains visible for the angler, much like an X Caddis with its prominent hair wing. Trout see the pattern as an opportunity to reach for a large insect that cannot flee before they swallow it.

Second, the fly floats very well compared to other emerger styles that also have bodies intended to sink. But I still find that the Harrop Green Drake emerger is best utilized in slow to medium currents. I would most likely choose a more heavily hackled fly, with a trailing shuck, that sits higher on the surface if I was fishing a choppy, boulder-strewn river section. Turbulent water tends to make flush-floating emergers sink quickly and can often make it near-impossible for anglers to see them on the water.

Fishing Techniques

Despite its flush-floating characteristics, Harrop's Hair Wing is surprisingly visible. Though you could fish this emerger in tandem with a larger, more high-floating Green Drake dun pattern (or a hopper or Chubby) to help you find it on the water. Tie the larger, more visible dry fly to your leader and attach the Harrop Hair Wing to the bend of that fly's hook using a clinch knot and 12 to 18 inches of tippet material. Make sure that the tippet material you're using is the same diameter as, or lighter than, what you used for the lead dry fly (tied to your leader) or the flies may twist and tangle, ending in a balled-up mess.

If you need to do so, you can also use finer tippets (5X and 6X) when fishing a Harrop's Hair Wing by itself, rather than the heavier 3X and 4X necessary to avoid the twisting that can occur while fishing large foam flies. The aerodynamic Hair Wing won't twist your leader like some of the other dry flies in this book. This can be important as the water drops and achieving good, drag-free drifts becomes more difficult with heavier tippets.

This stretch of water in the Lamar River has provided some of my most memorable Western Green Drake fishing. The moving water forces the trout to decide quickly if they want to eat a fly. And if drakes are hatching, they often eat Harrop's fly.

Reiner's Upside Down Drake

- **Hook:** #10 standard dry-fly hook
- **Thread:** Olive 8/0
- **Tail:** Moose mane
- **Body:** Olive hackle stem
- **Wings:** Hen hackles, tied Wally Wing style
- **Hackle:** Grizzly, dyed dark olive

Dean Reiner moved to the Yellowstone region from California in 1981, but he was born in Philadelphia and learned to fly fish on a stream running through his family's farm along the Pennsylvania–New Jersey border. Pennsylvania is one of the United States' trout-fishing meccas, and its inhabitants, current and former, have had an oversized impact on American fly fishing since its inception.

Between his stints in California and Montana, Dean was stationed in Vietnam as a Marine Corps helicopter crew chief in 1968 and '69. One of the most amazing stories about Dean Reiner is that he took his 9-foot 7-weight South Bend bamboo fly rod, which he got when he was eight years old, with him to Vietnam. Dean said, "Normally I didn't have much time to go fishing. But anytime I did, I went fishing." He'd fish the rivers when he could, for "shit-eating smelt." And he'd also fish the ocean with streamers for barracuda, near where he was stationed at Marble Mountain. But when he wasn't fishing, Dean was an American hero who survived seven helicopter crashes while fighting for his country.

Upside-down flies, like Reiner's Upside Down Drake (tied by Dean Reiner), aren't commonly fished these days. But they can sometimes fool the wariest trout that has refused other fly patterns.

Dean's South Bend fly rod endures today and is displayed on the wall of his fly shop, Hatch Finders, on the southern outskirts of Livingston, Montana. After listening to Dean's stories, I quickly realized that his old cane rod is a rare, special piece of our shared American history—something that should be hanging in the Smithsonian, if it wasn't on his fly shop wall.

Dean learned to tie flies, mostly on his own, with an old Thompson Model A vise. He told me that he "just looked at fly pictures and kept tying shitty-looking flies until they got better." But his flies today, including his intricately tied Upside Down Drake, are unabashedly beautiful. I asked Dean why he tied the fly with the notoriously difficult "Wally Wings." He said, "I did it because I could. But the fish don't really care. The fish aren't counting tails on our flies. It just looks like food, so they eat it."

As I stated earlier in this book, imitating large Western Green Drakes can be vital to catching trout in many of Yellowstone's fisheries from late spring into the fall. But if you're coming from the eastern United States, you might notice that Western Green Drakes do not look similar to the Green Drakes you're used to fishing. The Eastern Green Drake (*Ephemera guttulata*) is a completely different genus and species from Western Green Drakes (*Drunella* spp.), which means that Western Green Drakes are more closely related to eastern *Drunella* species like the *D. cornuta*, a fly many eastern anglers call a Blue-Winged Olive.

Fishing Techniques

Though Dandy Reiner (Dean's daughter) assures me that the Reiner's Upside Down Drake lands correctly every time, don't be dismayed if a casting error or sudden gust of wind causes the fly to land incorrectly. This can make the fly look like a crippled pattern, and I've caught many trout on flies that landed less than ideally when I presented them to trout.

The realistic-looking and beautifully tied Wally Wings that Dean incorporates into this fly pattern can cause your tippet to twist if your fishing material is too light. I try to fish these larger flies on 4X tippet and only go to 5X if the fish are obviously interested in the flies but are refusing to eat them. Try to keep your leader on the shorter size too, 9 feet and under, as this will often also help mitigate a potential twisting problem. There are few reasons to fish dry-fly leaders longer than 9 feet in the park, as the fish seldom require the same finesse anglers are trying to achieve by using longer leaders.

Reiner's Upside Down Drake is the kind of fly you keep for a special fish that's refused your other offerings. Its delicate wings and body create excellent fish-fooling qualities, but they come at the expense of durability. Dean told me, "It's not good for more than three fish. But I don't tie it for its durability. It's fun." Tie it to your leader when fishing drake hatches in Yellowstone, and you'll have fun too.

Most of the mayflies we anglers call Western Green Drakes are from the Drunella *genus, which means they are more closely related to Eastern Blue-Winged Olives than Eastern Green Drakes. Common names for aquatic insects usually lack a scientific basis, and they often cause confusion for anglers.*

- **Hook:** #8-12 TMC 5212
- **Thread:** Camel 8/0
- **Tail:** Wood duck fibers
- **Over-tail:** Caddis tan Zelon
- **Body:** Tan goose biot (look for long ones)
- **Hackle:** Golden brown CDC
- **Over-hackle:** Ruffed grouse back feather

Wollum's Brown Drake Emerger

Brown Drakes (*Ephemera simulans*) are one of only a handful of mayflies that are found throughout the continental United States. So if you've previously fished Brown Drakes anywhere in the country, you'll encounter the exact same bugs in Yellowstone National Park. Brown Drakes are large mayflies that can bring the biggest trout to the surface to eat them. But this hatch has a few drawbacks in the park. First, you won't find these mayflies in most of Yellowstone's waters, though the Upper Gibbon River and

lower portions of Slough Creek maintain fishable populations. Brown Drakes often hatch at dusk, which presents another problem since anglers are required to stop fishing the park at sunset. Finally, it's difficult to time the hatch. Brown Drakes tend to emerge in a concentrated window of around three days. So if you're not here in the week they appear, you'll have to wait until next year.

But in spite of these headwinds, Rick Wollum, the manager of Angler's West Fly Fishing Outfitters in Emigrant, Montana, has

Many park anglers who plan only to use dry flies miss some great fishing opportunities by not carrying wet flies, like Rick Wollum's Brown Drake Emerger. There are several ways to fish wet flies, and I've caught a lot of rising trout over the years by dousing them with floatant and using them as dry flies.

developed a beautiful Brown Drake wet fly that works very well in the park. Rick is originally from Denver, Colorado, but he's been living in Montana for the last thirty-five years. When he was ten years old, Rick read Joe Brooks's book *Trout Fishing*, and it inspired him to move to Montana, near Yellowstone. Rick knows the park well: He's been fishing it for forty-eight years, beginning when he was fourteen years old.

Rick told me that he began developing his fly around ten years ago to imitate Brown Drakes on the Missouri River, but he's been working to improve it ever since. He's a fan of legendary fly designer René Harrop's flies and said that his wet is somewhat patterned after a Harrop Brown Drake. Rick and I agreed about the difficulties of fishing Brown Drakes in the park. But he mentioned that a late June day with an evening thunderstorm to darken the sky can instigate the flies to hatch earlier than normal, providing anglers with a window to target them.

Brown Drake nymphs are burrowers that rise from the stream-bottom substrate to emerge in the surface film. So I asked Rick why he would use a wet fly to imitate them when most wets mimic insects that emerge subsurface and swim to the surface fully formed. I said that perhaps the fish take his wet believing it to be the nymph, wiggling as the dun tries to escape its shuck, and he agreed that could be possible. Rick also thought that it might imitate a drowned dun. That makes a lot of sense too.

Fishing Techniques

Rick told me that he fishes his Brown Drake Emerger wet, damp, and dry. That means he'll sometimes swing the pattern subsurface, like a wet, while other times he'll fish the fly "damp" right in the surface film. But he'll also use floatant to make the fly ride on the surface like a dry. I also fish my wets this way: I often use a powdered floatant, such as Frog's Fanny, and dust the flies so they float for at least a few casts. A wet fly's disheveled appearance just makes it appear buggy-looking. That can help fool some of the wariest dry-fly-eating trout.

Rick prefers to fish his fly with an intermediate sinking line (a line that sinks just beneath the water's surface) to rising fish. He told me, "I tend to cast the fly to where it's just slightly under tension, kind of drifting the fly, but not a hard swing onto the fish—I want a more natural drift. As those flies emerge, they're not swimming across the current. I have much better success not swinging the fly, just drifting it without a belly [a traditional wet-fly technique that drags the fly to the surface as the fly line pulls it] in the line."

Rick also ties his fly a little smaller (size 12 and 14) and "plays with the color scheme" to imitate the Hecubas (Drake Mackerels) that hatch in the park, most often in September. But wet flies can be used anytime. Fish will often eat them just because they look and behave (move) like real aquatic insects. And Wollum's Brown Drake Emerger can catch trout even in rivers and creeks that do not have a Brown Drake emergence.

- **Hook:** #14-18 Firehole Sticks 633
- **Bead:** Copper Firehole Stones round tungsten (3 or 3.5 mm)
- **Thread:** Chartreuse 8/0
- **Tail:** Dun mallard barred flank
- **Abdomen:** PMD turkey biot
- **Thorax:** Black Ice Dub
- **Legs:** Black Krystal Flash

Grobe's PMD Variant

My friend Matt Grobe, who lives in Bozeman, Montana, but is originally from western Pennsylvania, catches more large trout than any angler I know. One of the reasons he puts so many substantial fish in his net each season is because he's also one of the best nymph fishermen I've seen. So when I asked Matt to tell me about one of his favorite Yellowstone National Park flies, I wasn't surprised when he gave me a nymph.

Grobe's PMD Variant was created the same way in which most great fly patterns are envisioned: Matt was trying to solve a riddle for fishing a specific hatch on a specific river—PMDs (Pale Morning Dun mayflies) on the

Firehole River. When the park's long-awaited fishing season opens in late May, it's often anti-climactic. Most of the park's rivers and creeks are running too high, cold, and off-color to provide good fishing. This often leaves anglers, who've been dreaming during long winter nights about casting their flies among the bison and thermal vents, to target the park's lakes and ponds, which are less impacted by snowmelt. Or they travel to the Firehole, which is usually one of the few flowing-water fishing options at this time of year.

The Firehole is fed by hot springs, which raise its water temperature, making it a great early season option when the air is still cold.

Grobe's PMD Variant was designed to imitate Pale Morning Dun mayfly nymphs in the Firehole River. But you can also tie the flies in smaller sizes to imitate Blue-Winged Olives.

But these springs also ensure that the river will often get too warm to fish later in the summer when other park waters are at their pinnacle. The warm Firehole water often instigates aquatic insect hatches to commence earlier in the season, and that's the reason Matt targets PMDs on opening day—a hatch that won't begin in most park waterways until weeks later (or even longer).

Matt said he began developing his fly in Pennsylvania for the Sulphur hatch, which is very similar to the western PMD. "There would be a million guys fishing Sulphurs back there, so I would mess with patterns to come up with something different," he told me. "About four years ago, I hit a heavy Firehole PMD hatch on opening day. So I went to the heads of the riffles and started whacking fish. But I wasn't catching nearly as many as I should have; my Copper Johns [a popular nymph designed by John Barr] and other nymphs weren't hacking it, so I went home and did some PMD nymph research."

Matt settled on a fly with a biot body to provide a more realistic appearance. "That biot body takes more time [to tie], but it's much more productive if you fish high-pressured water like the Firehole in the spring. I firmly believe that the segmentation the biot creates is important. It's still slim, so you get a good sink rate, and it's just buggier than a thread fly." He continued, "I got the idea to use black Krystal Flash for the legs from another pattern, the Higa's SOS. But the real inspiration for the pattern came from my older brother and his flies."

Fishing Techniques

Matt is a proponent of tight-line nymphing techniques, which are often referred to today as Euro nymphing. Euro nymphing has been widely publicized in recent years because it's often employed in fly-fishing competitions, which have grown in popularity in the United States. This style of nymphing keeps you in tight contact with your flies and has been proven to be very effective in trout waters in the park and just about everywhere else. It's preferred by many of today's anglers over more standard nymphing techniques that usually employ a strike indicator to detect when a fish eats your sunken fly. Though you should know that many trout are caught with nymphs beneath indicators—that still works too.

Matt told me that even in years that are colder and snowier than normal, when the PMDs haven't begun to emerge as the fishing season opens, he still uses his PMD Variant on opening day. "Those nymphs will be moving in the riffles, getting ready to emerge," he said. One of Matt's park traditions is tying a dozen or so before his first trip. He said that tying the flies smaller, in size 18 and 20, will also work well for imitating little Blue-Winged Olives in the fall. He'll occasionally drop this smaller version from the bend of a small dry fly. A Blue-Winged Olive parachute or even a little Elk Hair Caddis would be a good dry-fly option. "I've had good luck fishing it in the Gibbon too at that time of year," Matt said. But if you fish Grobe's PMD Variant, you won't need luck to catch some trout.

The Firehole River is one of the park's best fishing options when the season opens in late May. Most of Yellowstone's other flowing-water fisheries are running too high and cold from snowmelt at this time to provide reliable fishing.

Jacklin's PMD Compara-dun

- **Hook:** #14-16 standard dry-fly hook
- **Thread:** Pale yellow 6/0
- **Tail:** Light dun hackle fibers
- **Body:** Dirty yellow beaver dubbing
- **Hackle:** Light dun, trimmed flush on the bottom
- **Wing:** Whitetail deer neck hair

Compara-dun style flies, created by my friend Al Caucci and his former writing partner Bob Nastasi (Bob has passed away), are some of the most common dry-fly patterns you'll find in fly shops. The reasons are simple: They work very well for imitating most mayfly hatches; they're relatively easy to tie; and they require only three materials in their construction—deer hair, Microfibetts, and dubbing.

The Compara-dun evolved from another fly pattern tied by New York's Adirondack Mountains fly-fishing legend Fran Betters. Mr.

Betters called his fly the Haystack. Haystacks share a couple common traits with Compara-duns: Both patterns have an upright deer hair wing, and they both utilize dubbed bodies. But Caucci and Nastasi replaced the Haystack's deer hair tail with more sparse-looking Microfibetts (similar to paintbrush fibers).

In general, Compara-duns look more refined than Haystacks. Compara-duns have uniform wings that stand straighter in relation to their hook shanks. Haystack wings are often tied to lean forward a bit, over the hook eye. And

This Jacklin's PMD Compara-dun (tied by Bob Jacklin) is an enhanced version of Al Caucci and Bob Nastasi's original Compara-dun. These flies are pattern styles, which can be used to imitate any mayfly dun by simply changing hook size and material color.

Compara-duns have tighter-wrapped, dubbed bodies when compared to the somewhat disheveled-looking Haystack. But be sure to note that Fran Betters's Haystack was purposefully tied to look disheveled and buggy, with its loosely wrapped body designed to trap air, helping it float. Both flies work very well, with Compara-duns probably having an advantage on flatter water, while Haystacks float a little better for riffles.

I carry Compara-duns to imitate every important mayfly hatch in Yellowstone, and they're often the only flies I need to get the job done. But if you force me to provide a little criticism of the pattern, it's that they are most effective outside of heavy riffles, where they sink more easily than heavily hackled flies. Perhaps West Yellowstone author and fly shop owner Bob Jacklin thought the same thing when he developed his Jacklin's PMD Compara-dun.

"I know Al Caucci, and I knew Bob Nastasi," Mr. Jacklin said to me over the telephone. "I began tying my Compara-dun after their book [*Hatches*]. I copied it from them, and I give them all the credit." But Jacklin's fly is different from a standard Compara-dun. And it's different for all the right reasons: Jacklin was trying to make it more useful for the rougher Yellowstone National Park waters he fishes, particularly the PMD hatch on the Yellowstone River. "It [the Yellowstone River] was the first place I fished in Yellowstone as a twenty-two-year-old right after I got out of the army. And it's still my favorite," Mr. Jacklin told me. But the Yellowstone is a very different river than New York and Pennsylvania's magnificent, but more placid, Upper Delaware River, which molded Caucci and Nastasi's Compara-dun.

"Compara-duns are great and I love them," Jacklin continued. "And my customers really like my version. They want it like you wouldn't believe." Jacklin's version adds hackle to the deer hair wing. This makes the flies float even better in rougher water, though he trims the hackle flush on the bottom so it also retains the ability to fool fish in flatter water. Jacklin told me, "The key is using the right hair for the wing. I use the neck hair from a whitetail deer. It's hollow and it really floats. I added the hackle to make it float even better, and it does."

Fishing Techniques

Compara-duns are most often fished to rising trout in flatter water and less turbulent riffles.

I usually fish these flies on 5X or 6X tippet. I prefer the 5X, if the fish let me do that. I'll know it's fine if they're eating my flies. But I'll often lengthen my 9- or 12-foot 5X leader with a couple feet of 6X tippet if the fish are being particularly critical, usually in slow pools in big rivers. My preferred approach with nearly all mayfly hatch-matching dry flies is to present the pattern from a position upstream of the rising fish, utilizing a reach cast to get the best quartering downstream, drag-free drift possible.

Pale Morning Duns (PMDs) are one of Yellowstone's most important mayfly hatches; they are the western version of the eastern US Sulphur. Just like Sulphurs, PMDs can sometimes hatch in incredible numbers, giving trout ample opportunity to feed, but also making it more difficult to convince the fish to choose your fly.

Bob's Special Rusty Para Spinner Long Tail

- **Hook:** #10-14 Dai-Riki 285 or 1XL nymph hook
- **Thread:** Rusty brown 140-denier
- **Tail:** Three to six long, dark elk hair fibers from the mane of a bull elk
- **Body:** Dubbing, a rusty color that Jacklin mixes himself, or a rusty-colored turkey biot, tied very thin
- **Rib:** Brown heavy thread (silk buttonhole thread, if you have it)
- **Parachute post (wing):** White Antron or poly yarn, tied as a short post then flattened over the hackle and thorax
- **Hackle (used to imitate the wing):** One or two oversized grizzly hackles, tied parachute style with the concave side of the hackle facing up

Bob Jacklin also calls this fly a "Para-spinner." And after our time discussing the pattern during a phone conversation was cut short, he was kind enough to mail me a few printed pages that delve deeper into it. In them, Mr. Jacklin states, "The Para-spinner is a blend of two great flies: the parachute and the spinner. My idea was to use a parachute style fly to simulate the bulky wing of the spent Trico [and, eventually, other mayflies] with the addition of the post for high visibility. It worked very well." Jacklin first tied his fly over thirty years ago as a Trico spinner imitation for the Upper Madison River and Hebgen Lake, but the flies worked so well that he began to tie them for other mayfly spinners like Blue-Winged Olives.

Bob's Special Rusty Para Spinner (tied by Bob Jacklin) can be used to imitate any mayfly spinner by changing hook size and the fly's body color, though many mayflies turn a rusty shade when they transform from duns to spinners. Mr. Jacklin likes to fish this larger fly when the tiny Trico spinners are on the water.

They work for most other mayfly hatches too, many of which turn a rusty color in their adult or spinner stage.

Mr. Jacklin further explains, "I oversize the [parachute] hackle, so it really represents the fly's wings. I'll split the tails with a dubbing ball, if a customer wants that. But I prefer a clump of elk hair for floatation. A lot of times, if the trout won't take what you're offering, put on a Para-spinner. They'll eat that. One of my tricks is to fish it with a Trico spinner in the summer. The fish just see this big spinner on the water and they eat it."

A "spinner" (its scientific name is imago) is the final mayfly life stage. After mayfly sub-adults (sub-imagoes), called "duns" by fly fishers, hatch from their water-living nymphal bodies, they usually fly to streamside vegetation to transform into spinners.

Many species turn into a rusty red color, similar to Bob Jacklin's Rusty Para Spinner presented here, but PMDs are often tan or deeper yellow as spinners. Male spinners are usually

Trout-fishing opportunities in Yellowstone National Park, from famous streams flowing near roads to backcountry adventures, are legion. But West Yellowstone icon Bob Jacklin told me that the first park river he fished is still his favorite. It's easy to see why anglers love the unique Yellowstone River.

the first to arrive and they gather in clouds, often over riffles, waiting for the females to appear. The males and females mate, and the males most often fly away from the stream. But the females return to the water to lay their eggs and then die, often floating on the water "spent" with their wings outstretched.

But how does knowing any of this help you catch more trout in Yellowstone National Park? To have mayfly spinners, you have to have mayflies that have been hatching before you arrive streamside. So if the fish have been selectively feeding on caddis or stoneflies, they may completely ignore your spinner imitation. But not always. You can try fishing a spinner imitation to any actively feeding trout at any time.

Fishing Techniques

Spinners are almost always fished on a dead drift to previously identified rising trout. Anytime you see a fish rising subtly, just dimpling the surface as it eats, often in slack current areas—pools, back eddies, etc.—the fish could be eating spinners, and it's a reasonable idea to try a spinner fly pattern.

Because mayfly spinners on the water are either dead or nearly so, it's vital that anglers represent them with drag-free drifts because the real ones seldom move, other than an occasional last-gasp shudder. It's usually best to position yourself upstream of an identified rising trout to cast down to it, to get the best drift. Mr. Jacklin says that you want to "try to feed your line [and fly] into the fish's window and into the fish's mouth." That's best accomplished from a position upstream of the fish.

Note: For tying the flies, Mr. Jacklin recommends that you "add a drop of Krazy Glue to the center of the wing post, which will soak onto the hackle, thus cementing them together as a unit."

- **Hook:** #12-14 TMC 9300
- **Thread:** Gray 8/0
- **Tail:** Speckled Microfibbets
- **Abdomen:** Gray goose biots, ribbed with either brown Pearsalls silk floss or Ovale pure silk floss
- **Thorax:** Adams gray beaver dubbing
- **Wing case:** Gray Evazote foam
- **Wing:** Medium dun Zelon mixed with Hungarian partridge

Wollum's Gray Drake Spinner

Gray Drakes (*Siphlonurus* spp.) are found in Yellowstone Lake as well as several of the park's rivers and creeks, including Slough Creek. They generally prefer slow-gradient waters and back eddies, often living in areas with silty bottoms and weeds. Gray Drakes are most important to fly anglers in their nymph or spinner stages. That's because the nymphs often swim to dry streamside vegetation to emerge, outside the reach of trout.

But I have observed Gray Drakes emerging in-stream during high-water events on New York's Upper East Branch of the Delaware River. When I mentioned this observation to Rick Wollum, manager of Angler's West Fly Fishing Outfitters, while we were discussing his Gray Drake Spinner, he told me that he had witnessed the same thing in Yellowstone National Park on the Madison and Lamar Rivers as well as Soda Butte and Slough Creeks.

In spite of the potential to find Gray Drake duns floating on the water's surface, most anglers agree that the best Gray Drake dry-fly fishing is usually to the spinner fall, as the

Spinners imitate the final mayfly life stage. These dying insects generally lie flush on the water's surface, making fly patterns tied to imitate them difficult for anglers to see on the water. The foam added to Rick Wollum's Gray Drake Spinner helps the fly float a little higher on the surface, improving its visibility.

females are collapsing to the water's surface after laying their eggs. While many mayfly species lay their eggs in riffles, Gray Drakes generally prefer to deposit theirs in the same slow-water areas where they lived as nymphs. The flies then float lifeless on the surface, where they are often eagerly consumed by rising trout. Wollum's Gray Drake Spinner is an ideal pattern to imitate these flies.

I think that Rick's fly's most important feature is the foam he uses around the wings. It helps the fly float a little higher on the water, making it easier for anglers to see it. Rick told me, "I've been playing around with the foam back, sort of a morph of the Craig Mathews Gray Drake spinner." He also uses Hungarian partridge feather fibers in his pattern's wings to suggest the venations in real mayfly wings. "I don't know if it makes a difference," he told me. "But I'm tying flies for myself as much as the fish."

Rick is an observant fisherman. He often takes photos of the aquatic insects he finds to compare them to his fly patterns, striving for as much exact imitation as possible. It's this desire that prompts Rick to mimic the Gray Drake spinner's split tails with his fly. "I use the Hockling Method to split the tails," he told me over the telephone. The Hockling Method uses a piece of thread, doubled over at the bend of the hook, to facilitate splitting the tails. "As you pull the thread up and over the body, it gives tension to hold the split tails in their place. It makes it much easier to divide the tails," Rick said.

Fishing Techniques

Just like Bob Jacklin's Special Rusty Para Spinner, discussed previously, you want to fish Wollum's Gray Drake Spinner on a dead drift, without drag, usually to fish that are already rising to eat natural Gray Drake spinners. I usually use a 9-foot 5X leader to do this. I nearly always cast to the fish from a position upstream of them, employing a reach cast to ensure that the fly reaches the fish before the tippet and leader, floating without dragging for as long as possible.

Rick told me that he generally expects to find Gray Drake hatches and spinner falls occurring in the Lamar River drainage a little later in the year than those in the Madison River inside the park. During years with high water, he said that you should look for fish rising to the spinners primarily in back eddies and even areas of flooded pasture along the rivers.

Rick also ties a version of his spinner to imitate Western Green Drakes when he fishes the Upper Yellowstone River in the park. For this pattern, he uses moose mane fibers for the tail because they closely match the natural's dark-colored tails. "I follow a lot of René Harrop's fly patterns," he told me. "But I use observation to develop my own flies." That's what makes Rick's fly patterns unique and effective.

Sparkle Dun

- **Hook:** #8-24 standard or 2XL dry-fly hook
- **Thread:** 8/0, color to match body
- **Tail:** Zelon, most often brown
- **Body:** Synthetic or beaver dubbing, color to match mayfly you're imitating
- **Wing:** Natural deer body hair

Craig Mathews (see also the X Caddis) details the history of his ingenious dry-fly creation, the Sparkle Dun, in a YouTube video made in conjunction with Umpqua Feather Merchants. In it, he says that he and his good friend John Juracek were fishing the Henry's Fork in the early 1980s for "super-selective, big rainbow trout that were sipping Pale Morning Dun [PMD] emergers." He continues, "One day we're on our hands and knees and we're watching these big fish feed, and it dawned on us: Every crippled and impaired dun that they took, the shuck, the trailing shuck, was shimmering and sparkling in the light. So we went back to our old fly shop, Blue Ribbon Flies in West Yellowstone, and located some sparkle material, sparkle poly, tied some flies—a Compara-dun, basically, style fly with a trailing shuck—went back the next day and just had tremendous success."

The Sparkle Dun is probably my favorite dry fly for imitating mayflies on flat water. But like Mathews says in his video, the Sparkle Dun looks similar to the Compara-dun, created by

Craig Mathews and John Juracek's Sparkle Dun is one of my favorite mayfly imitations. The trailing shuck tells trout that this mayfly is trapped and will still be on the water's surface when they rise to eat it. Though the fly pictured here is intended to imitate the predominately stillwater-living Callibaetis mayfly, you can imitate any mayfly species by changing hook size and material color.

Al Caucci and Bob Nastasi, which they derived from the Haystack by New York State's Fran Betters. I do not know Mr. Mathews personally, but it's been my great privilege to know Caucci, Nastasi, and Betters from my time living and working in the fly-fishing industry in upstate New York.

Perhaps the greatest attribute of all three of these imaginative tiers' fly patterns—the Haystack, Compara-dun, and Sparkle Dun—is that the flies are easy and inexpensive to tie. All you need is a tailing material, dubbing, and good deer hair for the wing. By changing hook size and material colors, you can effectively imitate all of the park's most important mayfly hatches: Blue-Winged Olives; Western March Browns; Pale Morning Duns; Brown, Gray, and Green Drakes; *Callibaetis*; and Tricos. Even the western *Epeorus* species, known as Pink Alberts or Western Cahills, can be imitated if you omit the trailing shuck, since these flies emerge fully formed from the stream bottom.

Though the materials used to tie the flies are few, the quality of these ingredients is paramount. Some fly shops carry cheap, poorly tied flies made overseas, though some foreign-tied flies are excellent. Often, poor-quality hair is used on the cheap flies, and there's not enough of it. These flies will float poorly and

This angler is fishing ideal Sparkle Dun water—water that is moving but not so heavily that it would easily submerge a flush-floating pattern like the Sparkle Dun.

only do that for a brief period of time. I purchased the Sparkle Dun featured in the photo from Blue Ribbon Flies. And I can attest that the flies you buy from that shop, as well as Al Caucci's former shop, the Delaware River Club, are of the highest quality. But this isn't the case everywhere. So if you don't tie your own flies, make sure you're getting a quality product from wherever you're buying them, or you'll be disappointed. And that should never happen with a well-tied Sparkle Dun, Compara-dun, or Haystack.

Fishing Techniques

I generally fish Sparkle Duns and Compara-duns with 9-foot 5X leaders, though I'll often use a 12- or even 15-foot leader, tapered to 6X, if the mayflies I'm imitating are especially small (18s and under) or if the fish I'm targeting are exceptionally picky; this often happens in very slow, clear pools. But I've also had success using Sparkle Duns for the largest mayflies such as Western Green Drakes and Gray Drakes: The key, again, is using enough of the best-quality hair you can find for the wing.

I wrote a story for *Fly Fisherman* magazine many years ago about a fly tier named Jimmy Charron who worked for Al Caucci. Jimmy taught me to build Compara-dun (and Sparkle Dun) wings by placing the stacked deer hair with its tips extending towards the hook bend, then pulling smaller clumps (approximately a third) of the hair upright and wrapping behind it, to make it stand. You can make a thick, substantial wing this way—one that will float very well and lean, just slightly, over the fly's body, exactly like a real mayfly.

Note: I've found Sparkle Duns tied with all different colors of trailing shucks, but most mayflies turn a brown color when they are fully developed nymphs, just before they emerge. That's why I nearly always prefer brown, or other dark-colored, materials for my mayfly trailing shucks.

- **Hook:** #12-20 standard dry-fly hook
- **Thread:** Fluorescent fire orange 8/0
- **Shuck:** Brown Sparkle Yarn
- **Body:** Copper MFC Sexi-Floss
- **Wing:** White MFC Widow's Web
- **Hackle:** Mixture of one brown and one grizzly feather

Wiese's Copper Hazy Cripple

Walter Wiese is originally from St. Louis, Missouri, but he's been tweaking and designing trout flies in the Yellowstone region since 2001. Walter has a story much like my own (and much like many people in the fly-fishing business) as to how he came to live in the Yellowstone area and earn a living as fly-fishing professional. "It was supposed to just be a fun summer job," he said. Yet now, twenty years later, Walter is still tying and designing flies and guiding anglers in and out of the park.

Walter, like many production fly tiers, has strong opinions about fly design and what makes a pattern effective: "I almost never fish high-floating flies. I want my flies to float, but to float low on the water. I can't remember the last dry I fished that wasn't a cripple or emerger." "Cripple" is a not-so-politically-correct name to describe aquatic insects that are damaged and unable to fly quickly from the water. Trout will actively feed on these malformed flies when they're available, often due to windy, rainy, or unusually cold conditions that inhibit the insects' transformation from gilled nymphs living beneath the water to flying duns that breathe air. Trout focus on

Walter Wiese's Copper Hazy Cripple is an excellent choice for imitating emerging PMDs. But Walter also ties this fly in a purple version that is best used as a general attractor pattern.

cripples because they can see that the insect is struggling and less likely to waste their precious energy by flying away as they rise to eat it. Fly patterns that mimic this behavior have become very popular around the trout-fishing world, including Yellowstone National Park.

Walter ties his Hazy Cripple pattern in two primary colors: copper and purple. It's the purple version that lent the pattern its name: The Hazy Cripple is a crippled version of the famous Purple Haze parachute fly pattern, which is a common attractor pattern found in most western (and some eastern) fly shops. Walter says he lets the weather determine which fly color he fishes.

Walter told me on the telephone, "I fish the purple one when it's cloudy and the copper when it's bright and sunny. You know, the whole bright day, bright fly; dark day, dark fly [a well-known fly-fishing theory when it comes to pattern choice]." The Hazy Cripple works well as an attractor "when there's a few bugs around," says Walter. "And it's easy to see." He prefers to fish the flies during a sparse mayfly hatch, partly because he says his pattern is

For an overcast day, like the one in which this rainbow was caught, anglers should choose the purple version of the Hazy Cripple, according to Walter Wiese, rather than the copper version which is best used when it's bright and sunny.

often easier to see on the water than other dry flies intended to imitate the hatch exactly.

The tying recipe for any fly pattern is sacrosanct to its creator. And Walter believes that the fluorescent fire orange thread he uses to tie the Copper Hazy Cripple is vital. The color bleeds through and it's an important strike trigger to get the fish to eat the fly, according to Walter. The choice of hackle color is also important. Walter mixes one brown and one grizzly hackle (just like the hackle on the famous Adams dry fly), and he says, "There's just something about that [color mixture]. I've tied the flies with dun-colored hackle to match specific insects, and it just works much better with the brown/grizzly mix."

Fishing Techniques

The Copper Hazy Cripple is a very good imitation for the *Ephemerella dorothea infrequens* (aka Pale Morning Dun, or PMD) mayfly hatch in the park. Because cripples are trapped, unable to get out of the water's surface film, it's almost always best to fish them with a dead drift, floating the same speed as the water. I generally use a 9- or 12-foot leader with 5X or 6X tippet to fish these types of flies.

Richard Parks (owner of Parks' Fly Shop) told me that the Hazy Cripple is his shop's most effective PMD emerger. Eastern anglers may not be familiar with this vital western mayfly hatch, but then they might not be as inexperienced as they think. The scientific name for the PMD includes three names (called a trinomial): *Ephemerella dorothea infrequens*. But most mayfly species only have only two names: one for their genus and one for their species. PMDs have three because they are very closely related to *Ephemerella dorothea dorothea*, also known as the small Eastern Sulphur. And just as Sulphurs are one of the most important hatches to imitate in the East, PMDs are vital to western fly fishers.

Wiese's Bob Hopper

A nyone who's spent time fishing west-ern US trout waters during the summer months knows the importance of grasshopper imitations. The flies are often used in eastern waters too, but if you look at the myriad patterns available for sale in most western fly shops, you'll quickly realize that hopper pattern selection is taken to another level in the West. That's why there are several hopper patterns included in this book. And according to Richard Parks of Parks' Fly Shop, one of the most important for fishing Yellowstone National Park is Wiese's Bob Hopper.

- **Hook:** #10-14 1XL nymph hook
- **Thread:** 6/0, color to contrast with body in #14, same color as fur dubbing in #10-12
- **Underbody:** Tying thread for #14, Ice Dub for #10-12 (Walter also blends some acrylic fibers into this dubbing.)
- **Foam:** Sheet foam from a craft store or Montana Fly Company. Use a hopper body cutter to make the body, or just trim to shape with scissors.
- **Tails (only on #10-12):** One rubber leg tied in a V at the bend of the hook
- **Wing:** MFC Widow's Web (EP Fibers can be used as a substitute.)
- **Legs:** MFC Centipede or Sexi-Floss legs for #14, standard silicone rubber legs for #10-12
- **Eyes:** Walter uses a black Sharpie to add eyes unless the fly is tied with a dark foam that makes it difficult to see. For those patterns, he uses nail polish to make the eyes.
- **Hi-vis post:** 2 mm foam (Walter cuts the foam across its grain to make it as small as possible to cut down on bulk.)

July is generally an aquatic insect–imitating month in the park. But when the calendar turns to August, many of the park's anglers adjust their focus to imitating terrestrials, land-based insects, often with foam grasshoppers like Wiese's Bob Hopper.

Walter Wiese developed this fly pattern style in 2012. Some patterns are designed to be tied one way, with one color, and that's it. But they evolve into a pattern "style" when the flies are tied in different colors, with different materials, to offer different fish-strike-inducing triggers during various conditions. The Bob Hopper is a hopper style. Parks' Fly Shop carries the flies in about fifteen different color combinations, but Walter Wiese ties them in more than twenty. Why so many? Walter told me that each year the best color changes, for reasons known only to the trout. The original pattern was tied as a size 14 peach-colored fly, but in any year, size 10s and 12s, in varying color combinations, can make the difference between catching fish or not in Yellowstone National Park.

Walter prefers the smaller size 14s for use as a general searching pattern. But if you want to suspend a nymph from the pattern, in a dry-dropper rig (also known as a "hopper-dropper" when using a hopper pattern as the dry), then the 10s and 12s offer more buoyancy and are less likely to be pulled subsurface by the sinking pattern's weight.

Walter spent a great deal of time tweaking this pattern, including designing his own body cutters, which are pressed into foam sheets to form the fly's body. But if you're tying the flies for yourself, without access to Walter's cutters, you can create the bodies by trimming the foam to shape with tying scissors.

Walter says that tiers need to use superglue for holding the "stubby" wing butts in place and for tying the rest of the fly. He told me, "The glue is really important. The fly will fall apart otherwise." Walter also adds an additional rubber leg to the bend of the hook, tied in a V shape, on size 10 and 12 flies. The additional leg improves the fly's ability to float, and, according to Walter, "It pushes the stonefly button a little more." Which means that trout may also eat the hoppers believing them to be stoneflies. Stoneflies have two prominent tails, which grasshoppers do not have. When I asked Walter what makes his hopper pattern stand out from all the rest, he told me that it's the fly's buoyancy, visibility, and durability. "There's not a lot of failure points on the flies," he said.

Fishing Techniques

You fish the Bob Hopper just like any other hopper pattern (see the upcoming Old-School Hoppers chapter for more information). But I think the size 14 flies really shine later in the park's hopper season after the fish have seen too many giant foam grasshopper imitations. Subtly can be important. A small size 14 hopper can interest the fish during late summer/early fall low-water conditions when a much larger fly may repulse, rather than attract, a strike.

You can also fish the size 14 flies on thinner-diameter tippet (down to 5X) than you can with large patterns, which will often twist fine material. But I still like 4X for fishing the smaller ones.

My good friend Steve Huber casts to an ideal hopper-fishing bank on the Lamar River. The grass in which the hoppers live extends to the water here, making it easy for one to end up wet. And the water is deep enough to cover the largest park trout that will be eagerly waiting for a hopper mistake.

- **Hook:** #6-8 Dai-Riki 320
- **Thread:** Red 140-denier
- **Body:** Pink ribbed fly foam (2 mm)
- **Wing:** Bleached elk hair
- **Overwing:** Light gray or tan thin fly foam, folded back to form head, topped with orange fly foam for strike indicator (hi-vis portion)
- **Legs:** Speckled yellow Centipede Legs (medium)

Reiner's Pink Pookie

Who or what is a Pookie? The name has become synonymous with a pink foam grasshopper pattern in the Yellowstone region, but where'd it come from? To get the whole story, I headed to Hatch Finders Fly Shop, which is located in a small plaza tucked ideally between Livingston and Paradise Valley, Montana. You have to pass by this shop if you're traveling to Yellowstone National Park's North Entrance from Interstate 90. I'd been to the shop before—it's only about ten miles from my home—but this time I wanted to speak with Dean Reiner, a legendary Yellowstone region fly tier, owner of the fly shop, and the inventor of the Pink Pookie, to include his fly's story in this book.

Most days Dean's daughter, Dandy, a terrific fly tier in her own right, is the face of the operation now that her father has shortened his time there, usually holding court only for a few hours in the morning. Their shop is old-school in the most beautiful way. And it's on proud display on their business cards which state, "We tie every fly." That "we" is Dean and Dandy. The other shop-staff member is a ten-year-old Maltese (a small white dog) named

The Pink Pookie (tied by Dean Reiner) is Dean Reiner's and his Hatch Finders Fly Shop's signature fly. Pink hoppers, like the Pookie, are very effective for catching Yellowstone's trout.

Yuki. And if you're thinking Yuki rhymes with Pookie, you're getting closer to their pink hopper's origin.

Pookie was the name of Dean's favorite fishing partner, who also happened to be a small, white Maltese that sadly died about ten years ago. An old story on the Hatch Finders website even mentions Dean taking Pookie on a trip to his favorite stream in Yellowstone, Slough Creek, before being reminded by a ranger that dogs must remain within 100 feet of a paved road or parking lot.

The pink part of Dean's most famous fly began when a guide from Bozeman came into the shop one morning and asked if they had any pink hoppers. They did not. But Dean and his business partner, Koichi Kawai, decided to rectify that. So they each tied six copies of ten different pink hopper patterns and handed them out to their guides to let the fish review them. Dean says, "The reports the next day were favorable. Pink was very attractable to the trout."

The duo then went about taking the best fly pattern elements, favored by their guides, from each of the flies—foam for improved floatation, rubber legs, etc.—and transformed them into one pattern, which ultimately became the Pink Pookie. But how did the dog's name get attached to a pink grasshopper fly pattern? Dean and Koichi didn't want to just call it a pink hopper—their website says there's no mystique in that. But after one of the flies fell to the ground and Dean took it from Pookie to stop her from being impaled by the hook, the dog begged for it, and in doing so, exposed her pink-hopper-matching belly. And the new fly pattern had a name.

Fishing Techniques

You fish the Pink Pookie by plopping it onto the water near grassy banks where a real grasshopper could fly or hop, or be thrown into the current by intense winds while trying to do either. Pink Pookies ride flush on the water's surface, and I think of them a little like a foam version of the Stalcup Hopper (see the Old-School Hoppers chapter).

One of the Pink Pookie's most obvious features is its color. For some reason trout seem to respond well to grasshoppers that are tied with body colors ranging from peach to pink. Remember the initial version of Wiese's Bob Hopper? It was a peach-colored fly too. Grasshoppers exist in a myriad of colors in the grassy meadows and sagebrush flats that line Yellowstone National Park's trout waters, though I don't believe that I've seen more peachy-pink ones than other shade variations. But why argue with success? The park's trout will change their preferred flies and the colors for those flies from time to time, but peachy-pink hoppers work well enough that I fish them every year.

The Pink Pookie's durability is another of its fine qualities. The Hatch Finders website says, "The fly is durable enough to stand up to every trout, and the only reason to change flies is if you lose it." The tiers at Hatch Finders should know: They tie every fly.

Yellowstone's trout love pink hoppers, and most fly shops near the park carry a multitude of pink hopper options. And though the Pink Pookie is one of my favorites, as you can see in this photo, other pink-colored hoppers also work well.

Old-School Hoppers: Dave's, Joe's, and Stalcup's

The importance of imitating grasshoppers when fishing the park in the summer months cannot be overstated. Many contemporary fly fishers choose patterns that look as realistic as possible; this often means using flies created with foam. Many of these foam flies have realistic-looking legs, wings, even eyes. This generally makes sense. If your fly looks as close to the real thing as possible, the fish will most certainly eat it, right? But after seeing so many of these flies, Yellowstone's trout often begin to look for something different—fly patterns that suggest imitation rather than force it.

Dave's Hopper
- **Hook:** #6-12 TMC 5262 or equivalent 2XL heavy hook
- **Thread:** Tan 100-denier G.S.P. (for its strength to spin deer hair)
- **Tail:** Deer belly hair or red hackle fibers
- **Hackle:** Brown, palmered over body and trimmed flush on top and even with hook gap on bottom
- **Body:** Yellow poly yarn (other colors like tan, green, and pink can also be used)
- **Wing:** Mottled turkey (optional to coat with flexible cement to increase durability)
- **Legs:** Trimmed and knotted hackle stems or knotted pheasant tail fibers
- **Head and collar:** Deer body hair, spun and trimmed to shape head

Dave's Hopper, created by angling legend Dave Whitlock, is an old-school hopper—a fly pattern created from mostly natural materials before the use of closed-cell foam became common. On any given day, oldschool hoppers can outperform the latest and greatest foam hoppers.

When this happens, "old-school" hopper patterns—those created from predominantly natural materials, designed before foam flies became common—can sometimes produce better results. The fish don't see as many of these older flies, since many anglers get caught themselves by new designs in their favorite shop's fly bins. That's the reason I fish Dave's, Joe's, and Stalcup's Hoppers later in hopper season.

Dave's Hopper was created by the famed fly tier and fisherman Dave Whitlock, one of fly fishing's giants and the writer of many important fly-fishing books and magazine articles. I've chosen to showcase Dave's Hopper in this section because his fly is probably the best-floating and most durable of the three I've included. According to the Midcurrent website, Joe's Hopper was created by Michigan fly tier Art Winnie but popularized by fly-fishing legend Joe Brooks; it's Mr. Brooks's first name that's attached to the fly.

Joe's and Dave's Hoppers have similar bodies. But the Joe's Hopper's head is formed with hackle, sometimes mixing two colors such as brown and grizzly, and it omits the Dave's Hopper's legs. The Dave's Hopper's spun deer hair head provides enhanced floatation for fishing riffled water, but I find the lighter, less bulky Joe's Hopper's profile to be slightly more productive in late summer's low and clear water flows.

The Stalcup's Hopper, which may be my favorite of the three, was created by the very talented and creative fly tier Shane Stalcup, who died tragically early in 2001 at the age of forty-nine. Mr. Stalcup is best known for his book *Mayflies: "Top to Bottom"* (Frank Amato, 2002) and his many VHS tapes and DVDs about fly tying and fishing. I consider his fly to be an intermediary pattern, designed with both synthetic materials (body, legs, underwing, and hi-vis post) and natural materials

(deer or elk body hair head and deer hair wing tied bullet-style). The Stalcup's Hopper floats flush on the water's surface, which makes it a little more difficult to see when tied in smaller sizes. But the park's trout love it. The pattern's only drawback is that trout teeth often tear it after a few fish, making it the least durable of the three.

Fishing Tactics

I generally fish "old-school" hoppers with a dead drift, the same speed as the current, just like foam hoppers. I cast these flies onto the water with a gentle, but intentional, plop to imitate the disturbance made when a real hopper accidentally gets wet. Sometimes real grasshoppers just lie on the water, like they're not really sure how they got there, but they often kick and squirm as they try to get out. The trout notice this struggle, and you can sometimes inspire a strike by gently pulling on the fly line to make your fly shudder and twitch. I generally fish these flies with a 9-foot leader, tapered to 3X or 4X tippet, either by themselves or in tandem with a nymph or small dry-fly dropper.

Joe's Hopper (top) and Stalcup's Hopper (bottom) are two more old-school hopper variations that have caught a lot of Yellowstone trout that ignored more high-floating, anatomically correct foam flies.

Psycho Prince

- **Hook:** #12-18 1XL or 2XL nymph hook
- **Bead:** Copper, gold, or black
- **Thread:** Black 6/0
- **Tail:** Goose biots, most often brown
- **Body:** Peacock herl or synthetic dubbing, most often green, orange, purple, or blue
- **Rib (optional):** Copper, silver, or gold wire, counter-wrapped
- **Wing case:** Goose biots, most often white
- **Wing:** Clump of yellow synthetic fibers, such as Flashabou
- **Head:** Synthetic dubbing, purple or color to contrast with body

It's nearly impossible to read a "how-to" fly-fishing guide for Yellowstone without encountering a mention of the Prince Nymph. The Prince Nymph was invented by California's Doug Prince sometime in the late 1930s or '40s. The pattern has evolved through multiple iterations during its long history, but the version most anglers know today usually has an optional gold bead head (or it's tied without a bead), a tail made from divided brown goose biots, and a wing case formed from white goose biots, which lie over the top of a shimmering peacock herl body. The fly also has a brown hackle collar, tied swept-back over its body. This "standard" Prince Nymph is the one that Yellowstone National Park master fly fisherman Richard Parks (Parks' Fly Shop) is fond of using beneath his Coachman Trude.

But the pattern is still evolving—a testament to the Prince Nymph's continued importance to fly fishing. More recent Prince Nymph versions such as the Prince of Darkness and the Psycho Prince have been created by substituting different-colored materials (often

You will find many versions of Doug Prince's original Prince Nymph in fly shops, but my favorite is the Psycho Prince. The only connection between a Prince Nymph and a Psycho Prince is the use of goose biots to form the flies' tails and wing cases.

synthetic) that are more durable than the easily broken peacock herl used for the original's body. The only thing that really binds these flies together as "Prince Nymphs" is the retention of goose biots for the wing case and tail.

The heaviest river trout I've caught in the western United States wasn't in Yellowstone National Park, but it wasn't far away either. That fish ate a size 18 purple Psycho Prince, trailed below a Perdigon, on a late winter's day in the Yellowstone River in Paradise Valley. The giant cuttbow was over 2 feet long and probably weighed somewhere around 6 pounds or so. But the flies also work well in the park. I often tie a small Prince Nymph, or one of its variations, to the bend of my guiding client's Chubby dry fly when we're fishing in the Lamar River watershed. Occasionally, a particularly gutsy cutthroat will obviously eat the Chubby on the surface, but when the fish is in the net, it also has the Psycho Prince in its mouth. But most often, a trout eats one or the other, with the Chubby sinking or pausing to indicate that the nymph has been taken.

Fishing Techniques

It's usually best to begin fishing any nymph pattern near the stream bottom and to drift it through the water column at the same speed as the current: dead drifted. If you're using an indicator, mend your fly line to keep the indicator floating ahead of it, the same speed as any foam, bubbles, or plant material you see in the water. You'll know if your fly is floating deep enough if you're catching fish and/or occasionally bumping, or getting stuck on, rocks and debris, making your indicator hesitate and occasionally sink. If you're getting stuck on most casts, your flies are likely too heavy. Remove or reduce any additional weight you've added such as split shot (remember, no lead allowed in the park). If you're using two flies tied in tandem without

This giant cuttbow ate a size 18 purple Psycho Prince. The fish wasn't caught inside the park, but it wasn't far away either. After the Yellowstone River exits the park, it flows through a valley north of Gardiner, Montana, through the Yankee Jim Canyon, and into Paradise Valley, where this magnificent trout was brought to my net. But lots of park trout are also caught on Psycho Prince nymphs.

additional weight, try removing the bottom one or switching to smaller or unweighted non-bead-head versions.

Prince Nymphs are attractor patterns, not always used to imitate a specific aquatic insect's behavior, so the best way to fish them varies. This gives anglers a lot of latitude as to how to use the flies, though, as I stated earlier, I usually begin by dead drifting a Prince Nymph. You can also try retrieving it by pulling short strips of fly line to give the appearance of a swimming nymph. Or dead drift the fly initially, after you cast and allow it to sink, then hold the line tight as it drifts below you (downstream) to intentionally make it drag from the stream bottom, imitating an emerging insect. But if you fish the fly this way, make sure you are using heavy tippet, 3X or 4X is preferred, because the strikes from a trout actively seizing a moving fly can be vicious and easily break the Prince Nymph from your tippet if what you're using is too light.

- **Hook:** #10-18 Firehole Sticks 317
- **Thread:** 8/0, color to match body
- **Weight:** Nontoxic wire (.010)
- **Tail:** Coq de leon fibers
- **Underbody:** Holographic tinsel (sometimes tying thread)
- **Overbody:** Materials vary depending on the pattern, but synthetic tinsels and feather quills are common.
- **Head:** Bright red thread, coated with epoxy
- **Wing case:** Black marker, coated with epoxy

Perdigon

Perdigon nymphs are one of the most effective patterns to be derived from competitive fly fishing. The FIPS-Mouche organization, which creates the rules for international fly-fishing competitions, has legislated that no additional weight be allowed outside of the flies. In other words, no split shot or other heavy materials are allowed to be attached to the leader. All weight must be incorporated into the flies. This has led to a great deal of experimentation from international competitors.

According to a *Fly Fisherman* magazine article written by Charlie Craven, the Perdigon style was invented by the Spanish fly-fishing team but popularized by the French. I have no idea why the Spanish didn't make it popular; maybe they were smart enough to keep it quiet, because Perdigon nymphs are deadly effective. The flies are usually tied with bead heads on barbless competition hooks, though you can sometimes find them on small jig-head hooks as well. Everything

Perdigon nymphs are designed to sink quickly, so anglers often do not need split shot to use them. The flies are most often tied on barbless hooks, making them legal to fish in the park. You can tie Perdigons in hundreds of colors, but the pearl one pictured here is one of my most productive for fishing in Yellowstone.

about Perdigons is designed to make them sink quickly and deeply.

Perdigons are formed with a taper, from their bead head to their wispy coq de leon fiber tail. This facilitates their ability to sink, and is most likely the key to their success: Lighter, non-tapered nymphs are often pulled over a trout's head by swift-moving water currents, but Perdigons are built like mini-torpedoes to get them quickly into the trout's feeding zone and keep them there. The flies can be tied in many different colors, though they most often (but not always) include flashy, synthetic materials.

Perdigon nymphs have become my go-to flies for fishing subsurface for trout everywhere, inside and outside Yellowstone National Park. They are an ideal companion when fished beneath a big Chubby in a dry-dropper tandem rig. Though the flies have received a good deal of press lately, I'm still surprised how few anglers fish them. Trout can get accustomed to seeing a fly pattern style and, over time, that style can lose some of its effectiveness. So I paused for a moment before I decided to add to their popularity by including them in this book. That alone should at least make you consider tying one to your leader for your next Yellowstone fishing trip.

Fishing Techniques

Perdigons should be fished, most often, drag-free and tumbling along the stream bottom. I'll also use them as the lead fly in a two-fly nymph tandem rig where the Perdigon's primary purpose is to get a smaller, lighter nymph pattern to sink more quickly. You can also accomplish this with split shot above a fly, but by using the Perdigon you give the trout another option for something they may eat. And often they eat the Perdigon.

Color can sometimes be a deciding factor in whether a fish eats your Perdigon, but I don't

think exact color matters. There have been times where I've switched from a bright, shining Perdigon to one with more muted, natural shades of brown and copper and began to catch fish. This seems particularly true on bright, sunny days when the water is clear. Sometimes the bright flash from a Perdigon tied mostly with reflective, synthetic materials can actually repulse trout rather than attract them. So if the fish aren't eating your bright, bottom-bouncing Perdigons, try switching to a more natural-colored one.

Perdigon size can sometimes be important for catching fish, and the most popular sizes are probably 12 through 16. I generally have more success fishing large Perdigons than I do smaller ones (size 12 seems to be the sweet spot). Perhaps it's because a larger fly is heavier and sinks more quickly, or maybe the reasons are known only to the trout. But even when I've fished two identical Perdigons with one smaller and one larger, the fish tend to eat the bigger one.

I caught and released this magnificent 26-inch brown trout on a Hot Spot Pheasant Tail Perdigon (my second-favorite color after the pearl) in the park on October 2, 2021. I was fishing the Perdigon with 4X tippet tied in tandem with the pearl Perdigon featured in this chapter. What makes this fish truly remarkable is that it's a pure river fish that didn't run from a lake to spawn. You never know what you might find in Yellowstone.

Grillos' Hippie Stomper (aka Holo Humpy)

- **Hook:** #6-18 Tiemco 3761
- **Thread:** Black 70-denier
- **Tail:** Moose body hair
- **Overbody:** 1 mm foam (often black) over top of 1 mm foam colored to match underbody
- **Underbody:** Holographic Flashabou or other flashy material
- **Wing:** Dun or white McFlylon
- **Legs:** Barred round rubber (fine)
- **Hackle:** Grizzly

It's fashionable these days for fly inventors to give their creations a funny, dirty, or otherwise memorable name. It makes sense. Fly designers want to get signed to one of the major fly-tying companies like Umpqua, Montana Fly Company, or Orvis to have their patterns reach a wider audience—and also so they can get paid. A catchy name helps people—fly company execs, anglers—remember the pattern, maybe even more so than the way it looks or the fish it catches.

I don't know anyone who didn't chuckle the first time they heard the name Hippie Stomper, designed by Andrew Grillos. But perhaps everyone didn't find it as funny as my circle of friends because the pattern is now sometimes called a Holo Humpy, a more politically correct alternative. For the record, I've seen flies with potentially much more offensive names than this one widely circulated. But that's OK.

Holo Humpy is an accurate moniker, as the fly sort of resembles a Humpy in a modern art sort of way, with foam pulled over its back instead of the Humpy's deer hair. And the Hippie Stomper does have a holographic body, so the "Holo" part seems to be appropriate too.

Whether you call this fly a Hippie Stomper or a Holo Humpy, you should carry some in your park fly boxes. I tend to fish Hippie Stompers after the park's trout begin refusing Chubbies and hoppers.

I'm certain that you don't have to feel disdain for hippies to appreciate this fly's beauty and effectiveness. And I'm fairly certain that no hippies were harmed during its manufacture. Call the fly whatever you want (as long as you give Mr. Grillos the credit), Yellowstone's trout just like to eat it.

You can find Hippie Stompers in a wide array of colors, ranging from size 6 all the way down to 18. All of them will work at some point in the season. I generally begin with the largest ones when the water's high and the big stoneflies are beginning to appear. I then work my way down to smaller ones in late summer when the fish are refusing larger foam patterns. But I think size 12 is my favorite.

The Hippie Stomper has a couple attributes that should place it in your fly box for Yellowstone National Park. First, it's durable. I think I might still have the first Hippie Stompers I purchased, though they are a bit pockmarked by trout teeth puncture wounds. Second, the flies are visible. It really doesn't matter how many trout eat your dry flies if you can't watch it happen—both for the coolness of visualizing a trout rise to your fly and for knowing when to set the hook.

Fishing Techniques
I generally use the Hippie Stomper as a searching pattern in the park, beginning after the fish stop readily eating my Chubbies and during, and after, midsummer when I'm often fishing hoppers. I really like the Hippie Stomper in the period when the trout begin to grow weary of hopper patterns and start eating other smaller terrestrials, and attractor dry flies, with more regularity.

The Hippie Stomper works well as a stand-alone dry fly, but is also very effective, particularly in sizes 12 and larger, as the lead dry fly in a dry-dropper rig. Cast the fly along drop-offs near the bank, through riffles, and around in-stream structure such as boulders. But fish it along deep water drop-offs in the center of slow pools too. I've caught a lot of cutthroat trout throughout the park by fishing this fly in those areas.

Be patient when a cutthroat rises to your dry fly. It's common to see them slowly ascending towards the surface and your fly, and it's easy to get antsy and blow the hook set by lifting your rod tip too soon. Make sure the trout eats your fly and begins to descend back to where it came from before you set the hook. This slow-motion feeding is one of the cutthroat's best ways to avoid getting hooked. And it seems like I pull too quickly on the first fish that eats my fly in the park every time I'm out there.

If you're interested in tying the Hippie Stomper, Mr. Grillos has a great video that shows you exactly how to do that on his website, andrewgrillosflyfishing.com.

- **Hook:** #8-14 2XL dry-fly hook
- **Thread:** 3/0 Monocord, color to match body
- **Underbody:** Fly foam (2 mm), often tan, pink, or black
- **Overbody:** Fly foam (2 mm), often black
- **Legs:** Round rubber
- **Hackle:** Brown or grizzly, trimmed to width of hook gap
- **Body:** Krystal Chenille, often black, tan, olive, or red
- **Underwing:** Krystal Flash, usually rainbow
- **Overwing:** Elk body hair
- **Thorax:** Synthetic dubbing, color to match body

Amy's Ant

Jack Dennis created the Amy's Ant approximately twenty years ago for his wife and former vice president Dick Cheney to use in the famous Jackson Hole One Fly contest. He named his winning pattern after his daughter. Though Dennis calls the fly an Amy's "Ant," it's obviously not intended to imitate any type of ants you'll find in Yellowstone National Park, or in any other US trout water—I think I'd quit fishing if I had to worry about running into real ants that look as big and menacing as the Amy's Ant.

Mr. Dennis's pattern is another large, high-floating dry fly that can be used to imitate a big stonefly, grasshopper, cricket, or cicada, but it's an attractor pattern that doesn't look exactly like any real insect. The Amy's Ant simply looks buggy enough that the trout will give it a try by eating it. And they often do that. I use this fly to show the fish something a little different if they're not responding well to my Chubbies or foam grasshopper imitations in the park.

The Amy's Ant is one of several productive fly patterns that have been widely circulated due to their success in the famous Jackson Hole One Fly contest. I like to fish the flies in the park to show the trout something a little different or to facilitate floating a dry-dropper rig in rough water.

Dennis demonstrates how to tie his creation online in a YouTube video by the Canada Northern Lights Trout Unlimited Chapter. In it, he states, "We've actually had 200 fish caught on this fly [meaning a single tied fly]. It's a very durable fly." And that is certainly one of the Amy's Ant's advantages. I can't remember one that fell apart while I was fishing it, though the foam sometimes gets pockmarked by trout teeth. But that's a good thing because it only happens if the fish are eating it.

If the fly has a drawback, it's that it's a rather complicated and time-consuming pattern to tie. And as Mr. Dennis says in the video, "If you cut the thread, the fly falls apart. There is no way of saving it." There are few fly-tying mistakes more frustrating than having a fly fall apart due to a tying mishap when it's nearly completed. This frustration is only magnified when it happens with a fly that takes a lot of time and materials to tie, like the Amy's Ant. But you can avoid that potential problem, if you want, by buying the flies at one of the many fly shops located in communities near the park's various entrances. Nearly all of them sell Amy's Ants.

Fishing Techniques

I fish Amy's Ants with a 9-foot leader and heavy tippet, preferably 3X. But many of my guiding clients are better able to cast these large, wind-resistant flies with a shorter 7½-foot leader, so shorten your leader if you're struggling to make accurate casts with an Amy's Ant. This is particularly common on windy days in the park. Like any large foam fly, you'll probably experience leader-twist problems if you use tippet that's too light, and a windy day can compound this. I never use tippet lighter than 4X for fishing the Amy's Ant.

You can also mitigate potential twisting problems that are caused by wind-resistant fly patterns by limiting your false casting as much as possible. This fly floats very well, and you shouldn't have to false cast it as much as other flies to help dry it—just backcast the fly from the water and lay it down. There's no advantage to cycling your cast back and forth (false casting); the fish can only eat a dry fly when it's on the water, and that doesn't happen while you're false casting. You also increase the chances of spooking a trout by constantly aerializing your fly line over its head. Many trout predators—ospreys, eagles, bears, humans—attack from above them. The fish are aware of this and often bolt for cover, or sink to the relative safety of the riverbed, if they are spooked from above.

The Amy's Ant is another very buoyant fly that's able to suspend some of the largest and heaviest nymph patterns while still floating. But like the other large foam flies in this book, it's also a fine option if you want to fish it as the lead with a small dry fly that you're having difficulties seeing on the water.

The heavy, turbulent water flowing into this pool will easily submerge most dry flies. In water like this, I like a buoyant, high-floating dry fly like the Amy's Ant.

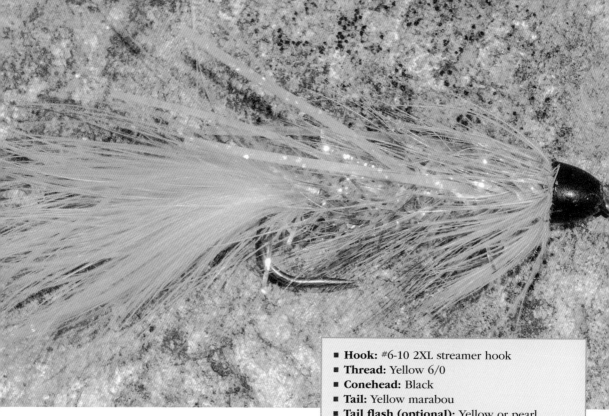

Yellow Yummy

- **Hook:** #6-10 2XL streamer hook
- **Thread:** Yellow 6/0
- **Conehead:** Black
- **Tail:** Yellow marabou
- **Tail flash (optional):** Yellow or pearl Flashabou
- **Body:** Yellow Cactus Chenille or other type of chenille with flash
- **Legs:** Pearl or yellow Sili Legs
- **Palmered hackle and collar:** Yellow hackle

Many fly anglers traveling to Yellowstone National Park are planning to fish dry flies. The park's often pastoral, crystal-clear waters, combined with its trout's eagerness to surface feed, can create perfect dry-fly-fishing conditions. But this isn't always the case. As the season progresses from its opening in late May through midsummer, the trout can become wary to rise for yet another floating fly after being previously hooked by them. But the park is huge, and fishing options are legion, so this isn't necessarily true everywhere. This midsummer dry-fly reluctance is particularly common in waters that are easily waded and located close to paved roads. So if you're casting your dry flies with little to no reaction from the trout, it's probably time to do something different: You can hike farther from a road, or you can try fishing a streamer.

Many anglers only fish streamers during high-water events like those found during runoff or after a heavy rainstorm. And they usually do so as a last resort. The prevailing thought: "The water is high and off-color, the sky is cloudy—maybe it's raining—and nothing has eaten my dries, wets, or nymphs, so

The Yellow Yummy is a simple rubber leg version of the Woolly Bugger. It's best attribute is its yellow color, which Yellowstone trout seem to find irresistible.

I guess I'll try a streamer." It's true, streamers can sometimes work during those conditions, and they're worth trying. But the park's trout, particularly its cutthroats, cuttbows, and rainbows, will often chase and eat streamers during conditions considered less than ideal by many casual streamer aficionados: low and clear water with bright sun.

The first Yellow Yummy I saw was lying in a dusty cabinet at a fly shop where I was employed. The Yummies were being removed from the streamer section by the store's owner, and added to the bargain fly bin, because they had been at the shop for years and few anglers purchased them anymore. The flies were inexpensive, so I bought a couple. During one slow morning while fishing the Lamar River, I decided to give the fly a shot. There was a deep cut in a side channel of the main river, formed by significant snowmelt-runoff erosion in the spring. It had to be near ten feet deep, and I could only see the bottom where it shallowed towards shore. But I could easily see the bright Yellow Yummy, strobing

Lenny Gliwa shows that the park's trout will eat yellow streamers (and other colors too) even when the water is muddy from a summer afternoon thunderstorm. Many anglers leave if they find dirty water, and that's not always a bad choice if you have other options. But you might be surprised by a good fish if you throw streamers in the mud.

through the deep water, after I cast it to the far bank and began stripping it back to me. Then I saw the fish.

Yellowstone cutts, two and three at a time, came charging into the bright summer sunlight pursuing the fly like they only feed on Yellow Yummies. I don't know what the park's trout think the Yellow Yummy imitates. Perhaps its rubber legs make it look like a Golden Stonefly nymph—there are lots of those in the park. I think the pattern's best attributes are that it's shiny and yellow. For some reason, I've found that Yellowstone trout respond better to yellow streamers than any other color.

The Yellow Yummy is just one of many different streamers that are based upon Pennsylvania's Russ Blessing's Woolly Bugger (see the Woolly Worm chapter in this book). That fly was initially designed as a hellgrammite pattern (the larval form of the dobsonfly), but by tinkering with its design, you can make it look like a lot of trout foods, from crustaceans to aquatic insects to fish.

Fishing Techniques

The key to finding productive streamer fishing during the summer is locating pockets of deeper holding water when most river and creek sections are low and clear. Once you find a good pool or pocket to prospect with your Yellow Yummy, begin by casting it towards structure; this could be a boulder or downed tree, but in places like the Lamar River, it may only be deeper water along a high bank. Strip the fly as soon as it hits the water. The trout will guide you to what happens next: If the fish eat your streamer, great! Keep fishing through the deep pocket. But if they only flash at it and refuse to eat it, strip the fly faster to attempt to elicit a predatory strike, or pause the fly after you strip it. That sometimes works in the park. But if it doesn't, change flies or move on.

Steeves' Cow Killer Ant

- **Hook:** #12 standard dry-fly hook
- **Thread:** Black 6/0
- **Abdomen/head:** $\frac{1}{16}$-inch foam, cut into disks. Use a larger disk for the red abdomen than the one used for the black head.
- **Body:** Peacock herl, dyed black
- **Legs:** Black Krystal Flash

What does a fly tier who was born in Alabama, and who still lives in the South, know about flies for fishing Yellowstone National Park? Well, trout are trout, and they tend to eat similar things wherever they live. But, ironically, Harrison Steeves fished his Cow Killer Ant for the first time not in the South, but in a side channel on Montana's Madison River, where it fooled six rising trout.

I got to know Harry, an amazing fly tier who specializes in foam terrestrial patterns, while guiding and running a fly shop in New York's Catskill Mountains. He would often successfully present his terrestrials to the Upper Delaware's ultra-selective trout when everyone else was struggling to catch them with Sulphur mayfly patterns.

Harry has a great YouTube video detailing how to tie his Cow Killer Ant. In it, he explains how this pattern received its name: "As a kid growing up in Alabama, we ran across these great big, what most people call velvet ants. They really aren't ants. They're wasps. Flightless wasps. And as kids we used to call these things 'cow killers' because we were convinced that if they ever bit a cow, the cow would die. So that's where the name comes from."

Harrison Steeves is one of the most creative terrestrial fly designers in the country. His two-toned Cow Killer Ant is one of my favorite summer terrestrial patterns for the park.

Though I had previous knowledge of Harry's pattern, my first experience fishing a Cow Killer Ant came during my initial western fly-fishing trip, organized by Simms (a fly-fishing gear manufacturer) and my former boss, Tony Gehman, owner of TCO Fly Shop. My fly shop colleague Steve Spurgeon and I were being guided down the Yellowstone River, just outside of the park near Gardiner, Montana. At the beginning of the float, our guide handed me a Cow Killer Ant, which another guide had told him was working well. It worked well for us too that day, and my first Yellowstone cutthroat trout and mountain whitefish were caught with the fly. I've been fishing it ever since.

The Cow Killer Ant's two-toned color makes it a little more visible than a mono-colored fly. Its black Krystal Flash legs give it a shimmering glimmer of life without being so bright that it causes trout wariness. The Cow Killer doesn't really look like any terrestrial found in nature, but it must look enough like trout food for the fish to eat it, because they do. This pattern can be very effective when most other park anglers are fishing hopper patterns in the summer. The fish see so many of those large

The run beside this rocky ledge creates the perfect opportunity to fish a terrestrial that might fall or fly into the water from the overhanging vegetation. I would drop a Cow Killer off the bend of a foam hopper and look for a cooperative fish in this spot.

flies that it sometimes seems like they actively search out anything that isn't a hopper.

Many Yellowstone National Park anglers want only to fish large dry flies. The reasons are obvious: Big dries are easier to see on the water, and there are few things more awesome in fly fishing than watching a big trout breaking the surface to eat a giant Chubby or large foam grasshopper. But because of this, the park's fish see a lot of these types of flies. And they can become reluctant to eat them, particularly as summer pushes into mid-August and September and the water levels drop. This is when you should be fishing the Cow Killer Ant.

Fishing Techniques

All terrestrial insects end up floating on the water by accident: They unintentionally fall, fly, or hop into it. The Cow Killer Ant looks a little like an ant but it also resembles a beetle, both of which crawl along streamside vegetation and sometimes fall into the water. You should generally fish this fly drag-free, the same speed as the current. But terrestrial insects that inadvertently end up on the water's surface don't want to be there, and they sometimes struggle to get out. This movement draws trout attention, and it's sometimes the key factor in provoking a trout to strike. So if you can see a trout that is showing interest in your Cow Killer Ant but won't eat it, you should try gently pulling on your fly line after the fly lands on the water to "twitch" the pattern, making it move just a little to give the appearance of life.

The two-toned nature of Cow Killers help you see them on the water. But as fly fishers age, and our eyesight often diminishes, these flies can still be difficult to locate. So when I, or one of my guide clients, struggle to see where my Cow Killer Ant lands in relation to my cast, I often fish it in tandem with a larger, more visible dry fly like a Chubby.

JoJo's Flav/Drake Mackerel

- **Hook:** #12-14 standard dry-fly hook
- **Thread:** Olive 6/0
- **Dubbing ball (to divide the tail):** Olive Hareline Super Fine
- **Tail:** Moose mane
- **Body:** Light olive Hareline turkey biot
- **Hackle:** Grizzly, dyed golden olive
- **Wing:** Light tan or white MFC Widow's Web

Joe Moore and his partners, Jonathan Heames and Justin Spence, are co-owners of Big Sky Anglers fly shop in West Yellowstone, Montana. This very modern shop and guide service has a strong historical connection to Yellowstone National Park because it was once owned by Bud Lilly. Mr. Lilly was a pioneering icon who was at the forefront of developing the fly-fishing industry in and around West Yellowstone and Yellowstone National Park.

Today, Joe Moore has become one of the region's most creative and respected fly tiers and pattern designers. His contributions continue to perpetuate West Yellowstone's status as one of the most important locations in the world for fly anglers. When I asked Joe to tell me about some of his flies for this book, he started with his JoJo Drake series. Joe's JoJo flies weren't created to imitate just a single mayfly species. They encompass a fly-tying style where many mayflies can be imitated by simply changing the color of the materials and the size of the hook used to construct them. You can find a lot of different options at Big

JoJo's Flav/Drake Mackerel was designed to imitate Drunella flavilinea *duns, often called "Flavs" or Lesser Green Drakes by anglers, as well as the Drake Mackerels (*Timpanoga hecuba*) that hatch in the park in September. But you can use this great fly pattern style to imitate most mayflies.*

Sky Anglers' shop that will cover everything from stillwater *Callibaetis* mayfly duns to the often rusty-red-colored mayfly spinners, as well as Green Drake patterns and others to imitate the park's most common hatches.

"The first drakes I tied in this style were designed for the larger ones that hatch in the spring," Joe told me. "Then I scaled it down for the Drake Mackerels [*Timpanoga hecuba*] that hatch in the park in September. Those drakes stand high on the water. It's like they're wearing high heels. So my JoJo Drake, with all that hackle, trimmed short, creates a lot of points of contact on the water [mimicking the way a real Western Green Drake stands on the surface]." Picky trout often search for specific fly pattern features. Their presence, or lack thereof, becomes the reason they do or do not eat a fly. Fly fishers call this a "triggering mechanism." And the trimmed hackle on the JoJo Drake Mackerel does that.

The park's earlier Western Green Drakes are in the *Drunella* genus (*D. grandis, D. doddsii*), but these hatches tend to end before the Drake Mackerels (often called "Hecubas" by anglers) begin. By this time in the season, the trout have probably already seen a lot of Green Drake dry-fly imitations, and they can become more difficult to catch during the Drake Mackerel emergence. Joe told me, "The fly is really visible, and it floats great. But if the fish get picky [because it's too visible], you can just cut the wing down a little bit."

Some of the best Yellowstone National Park Drake Mackerel fishing occurs at a time of year when there are fewer anglers on the water. The Lamar River and Soda Butte Creek maintain very good populations of these mayflies. But when they appear in September, the often-low water, combined with bright sunshine, tends to instigate their emergence later in the afternoon, continuing through the evening, when the sun gets lower in the sky. There aren't a lot of dining options in Yellowstone, and many vacation-visiting park anglers are headed out for their evening meal this time of day. This opens up more water for those who are willing to stay, fish, and grab a late dinner.

Fishing Techniques

The angler-driven hype surrounding Western Green Drakes may not reach the hysterical levels of Eastern Green Drakes (which are a completely different mayfly genus and species—*Ephemera guttulatta*), but they can provide fantastic dry-fly fishing that many anglers eagerly pursue. These mayflies are large insects, and the park's trout become keenly aware of their presence not long after they begin to emerge.

If the drakes have been appearing on park waterways for a few days, it can be very effective to fish the water by blind casting drake patterns, such as JoJo's Drake Mackerel, even if you're not finding trout immediately rising to the naturals. In the spring, I'll often fish a drake pattern as the dropper fly, behind a Chubby, in a two-dry-fly dropper rig. For the September Hecubas, I fish the same rig but substitute a foam hopper for the Chubby.

Autumn in the Lamar Valley, and nearby Slough Creek, can provide excellent fishing opportunities for hatches of Drake Mackerels, often called "Hecubas" by anglers after their species name.

JoJo's Ant, Black

- **Hook:** #12-16 standard dry-fly hook
- **Thread:** Black 6/0
- **Tail:** Black MFC Widow's Web
- **Underbody/head:** Black foam, with its butt tied down along the hook shank, then pulled forward to form a humped body and small head
- **Body:** Black Ice Dub, wrapped over the foam underbody
- **Legs:** Medium brown MFC Barred Sexi-Floss (small)
- **Wing:** Light tan or white MFC Widow's Web

As I stated previously, terrestrial flies—those that hatch on land and not in the water—are vital for catching trout during Yellowstone's summer months. Joe Moore's JoJo Ant is a great pattern to use when the fish begin to refuse larger foam Chubby and grasshopper patterns. "I originally tied this fly back in 2004," Joe told me. "But it had an elk hair wing. I changed the wing to Montana Fly Company's Widow's Web material several years back."

"My black ant is really good. But I might like the red/black version even better," he said. I agree with Joe, as there often seems to be a trout triggering mechanism that encourages fish to eat two-toned terrestrial patterns a little better than single-colored flies. Maybe it's because so many real terrestrials have multicolor shades within their bodies. Or perhaps it's because trout visualize a two-colored fly a little differently. But just like the red and black Cow Killer Ant that was discussed previously, these flies work very well. That doesn't mean you should never use all-black terrestrial patterns in Yellowstone—I've caught many

The JoJo's Ant, shown here in an all-black option, is a good terrestrial searching pattern for late summer and fall fishing in the park, though Joe Moore, the pattern's creator, prefers the fly tied in a red/black version.

fish on patterns like that. And on days where there's a lot of sun glare on the water, an all-black fly can be easier for an angler to see than a lighter-colored one.

When Joe and I were discussing his fly, I asked him why he sometimes incorporates light tan-colored Widow's Web into its wings, when many other tiers opt to go with white due to its increased visibility. "I think white can be too bright when the fish in the park get pressured and picky," Joe said. "The light tan is just a little more subdued, but you can still easily see it. It's just not as obnoxiously white." Trout often become more selective when they feed as the season wears on; angling pressure and low water tend to make the fish more distrustful.

The JoJo's Ant is a midsized dry fly, usually tied from size 12 to 16. You'll find many terrestrials in the park that are much smaller than that. But the JoJo's Ant is a visible pattern, and

Yellowstone National Park has many different terrestrial, or land-based, insects, which its trout actively pursue as aquatic insect hatches diminish later in the fishing season. Some, like this Mormon Cricket sunning itself on the path to Slough Creek's Second Meadow, offer a substantial food source for the trout.

that's a great aid to the angler. I'll fish a JoJo's Ant as the lead fly with a smaller, less visible dry-fly ant, like a simple Fur Ant. Fur Ants are tied with two bumps of dubbing, one for a thorax and one for an abdomen, separated in the middle by black hackle to represent legs. This very basic fly works well, but it's extremely difficult to see on the water; I don't like to use it without the aid of a more visible pattern tied in tandem. This tandem also gives the fish options, and I'm often surprised at how often the park's trout choose the larger version in spite of the fact that the real ants they're targeting are much smaller. This is especially true during flying ant flights, which are common in the park in August and September.

Fishing Techniques

The JoJo's Ant is most effective during summer when aquatic insect hatches begin to diminish as a midday staple, and the fish look to feed more opportunistically on random insects. You can fish the JoJo's Ant along drop-offs near the stream banks, but I've also had success by drifting the pattern through shallow riffles where fish are seeking cover in diminished summer water flows.

I usually fish this fly with a 9-foot leader and 4X or 5X tippet, preferably 4X if the fish don't seem to mind. I try to use the heaviest tippet that still allows me to present the flies in an effective manner. Water temperatures rise during the summer months, making it more difficult for trout to procure the oxygen they need for survival. You can land fish more quickly by using heavier tippets, and this greatly enhances a trout's chance of survival. Even fish that are caught and released will sometimes die. It's best to do whatever you can—land them quickly, keep them wet, and be ready to take a quick photo if you choose to do that—to aid their survival.

Fat Head Moth

- **Hook:** #10-14 standard dry-fly hook
- **Thread:** Tan 6/0
- **Body:** Tan or gray beaver or synthetic dubbing
- **Rib (optional):** Gold tinsel or synthetic material
- **Underwing:** Tan or gray synthetic yarn such as Antron or Zelon
- **Wing/head:** Stacked and divided elk or deer body hair, trimmed short at the eye to form a head

Many anglers outside the western United States don't always consider using moth fly patterns when they're fly fishing for trout. Though I did write about the occasional importance of imitating Forest Tent Caterpillar moths for fishing New York's Upper East Branch of the Delaware in my book *The Fly Fishing Guide to the Upper Delaware River* (Stackpole, 2007), moth fishing isn't unknown in the East. It's just not as common.

The great diversity of eastern aquatic insect hatches, combined with more-common terrestrials—ants, beetles, crickets, etc.—are the flies generally imitated by eastern anglers. Plus, moths are cyclical. Some years their populations explode, and they can be found in abundance along localized eastern waters. Other years disease, human-spread insecticides, or predators keep their numbers in check, and there are far fewer of them. There has to be enough of them, and they have to actually get on the water, for trout to take notice. This usually happens only in years with a heavy moth infestation.

Moths aren't always considered an important trout food by anglers in the eastern United States. But Spruce Moths, which can be imitated with this Fat Head Moth fly pattern, are eaten by trout every year in areas where they're found within Yellowstone National Park.

But this isn't necessarily the case in the West. Spruce Moths are a famed emergence that many anglers plan to fish each season. These midsized insects are usually imitated with size 12 and 14 flies, but larger imitations (size 10) can sometimes help get the fish's attention. Though Spruce Moths are most commonly found from mid to late summer (July through September), the Fat Head Moth can be used throughout the park's fishing season because it also looks like a fluttering caddisfly. This makes the Fat Head Moth one of my favorite moth imitations.

Yellowstone trout are generally more-opportunistic feeders than those found in heavily fished trout waters near larger urban populations throughout the rest of the country. But don't think they'll just jump into your net. There are certain times, on certain park rivers and creeks, where the trout can become very picky and challenging to catch. Yellowstone hosts fewer angler days, due to its shortened fishing season, than many of the country's other wild trout regions, most of which now offer year-round angling options. The park's shorter season and reduced fishing hours (you can't fish before sunrise or after sunset), combined with more-difficult angler access (no one lives on these streams), ensures that the fish see fewer fly patterns than their brethren that live elsewhere.

This keeps the park's fish somewhat naive, at least compared to the average trout living in a famous stream outside the park; it's especially true in small, more remote, backcountry park streams and lakes that are often inhabited by brook or cutthroat trout. But there are some instances where Yellowstone's fish can be as fussy as trout found anywhere else in the world, making fly pattern selection crucial. It's often more productive to show these difficult trout a fly that they haven't been seeing on a daily basis rather than just tying on

whatever everyone else has been casting. And that's where a pattern like the Fat Head Moth can come in handy even if you're not seeing moths on the water.

Fishing Techniques

As their name suggests, Spruce Moths are usually found near coniferous trees. The moths are most active on early summer mornings, in the evening when the sun is setting, and into the night. They head for cover during the heat of the day. But remember, it's illegal to fish the park's waters after dark, so once the sun sets, you must quit fishing no matter how many fish are rising. Do you really want to be stumbling around the park after dark where things can eat you? Yeah, me neither.

I usually fish the Fat Head Moth on 4X tippet while prospecting (blind casting) for trout. I generally fish the fly on a dead drift, but if the trout are hesitant, it can also be skittered (purposefully dragged across the water's surface) or occasionally twitched by gently tugging on the fly line, to make it look alive.

Spruce Moths, as their name implies, eat conifer trees. If you want to find them in the park, you need to fish areas where evergreens grow near the water so the trout have the opportunity to eat them.

- **Hook:** #14-16 standard dry-fly hook
- **Thread:** Orange 6/0
- **Body:** The closed-cell foam butt overwrapped with orange thread
- **Shell/head:** Orange closed-cell foam, trimmed to shape
- **Legs:** Orange Barred Sili Legs

Long's Indicator Beetle

When one of your friends tells you about a fly pattern that really works well for them, you listen. When that friend's guide service is the only three-time winner of the prestigious Orvis Guide Service of the Year award (2003, 2004, 2015), you pay special attention, particularly when his guide service often works the same waters you do: the Yellowstone, Lamar, and Gardner Rivers and Slough and Soda Butte Creeks.

Matthew Long grew up in central Pennsylvania, not far from where I was raised. He's another on the long list of Pennsylvania transplants in this book that now call Montana home. When I asked Matthew to give me a pattern or two for the book, the first fly he grabbed was his Indicator Beetle. "I had one client that actually counted strikes [how many times the fish tried to eat it] on one of our trips. Two hundred sixty-seven times, in the course of one day's fishing, a trout rose to this fly. Of course, we only caught about thirty of them," he said with a smile. "It's generally a cutthroat fly—think northeast corner of the park.

Beetle fly imitations are often tied with black materials, which make them difficult for anglers to see on the water. But Long's Indicator Beetle is bright orange and a very good choice if you're struggling to see your black fly.

Though I've caught some big brown trout on it too, and the brookies in the Upper Gardner love it. But the fly doesn't work well until the water is clear and the temperature begins to get warm. Late July through early September is best. As soon as it warms up, it's on."

Beetle imitations sometimes take a backseat for anglers who'd rather fish grasshopper and ant terrestrial patterns. But that is a mistake. Beetles are one of the most prolific insects on the planet, and they are a very important food source for trout all over the world, including those in Yellowstone National Park. "But why fish an orange one?" I asked Matthew. "Why not use a more traditional black beetle?"

"I don't know. It works, just because it works," he said laughing. "It's visible, but you have to grease it to help it float." Matthew also ties the fly in a red version, and you could tie it with more-traditional black materials, but he says, "The orange is the ticket."

Though most anglers who fish beetle patterns tend to gravitate towards black ones, there's a good reason why orange is also productive. Real beetles come in all different colors, and some of the insects we don't always associate with beetles (ladybugs, for example) are at least partially orange-colored. The Indicator Beetle's bright color is also a great aid for anglers: It's much easier to see on the water than black versions, most of which have to include some sort of visible, fluorescent material on top to help you see it.

Fishing Techniques

Matthew prefers to fish the Indicator Beetle as a stand-alone pattern with 5X tippet, though he will occasionally use it to suspend a small nymph in a tandem rig—just make sure your nymph isn't too large and heavy or you'll have difficulty keeping the Indicator Beetle afloat. When Matthew does fish his beetle in tandem with another dry fly, it's nearly always with another size of the same orange beetle: a size 16 dropped off the bend of a size 14's hook. You generally want to use the smaller-sized fly on the bottom of a two-fly tandem to help facilitate your leader's ability to turn over.

"I fish it in the seam lines and along the edges. You know, where the fish are," Matthew laughed. But you should also fish this fly anywhere you'd fish any other type of terrestrial, where they can accidentally end up in the water during their daily searches for food and mates. I look for areas beneath tree limbs or along high grassy banks. And I generally fish beetle imitations with an intentional "plop" as they land on the water. You can make your fly plop by gently, but purposefully, casting it at the water's surface rather than aiming for a spot above the water like you would do with dry-fly patterns imitating aquatic insects. Just don't exaggerate the plop too much or you could actually spook a fish nearby when your fly line leader and fly slam into the water. And your fly will most likely sink if your plop is too aggressive.

Matthew Long says that his Indicator Beetle is a "cutthroat fly," and this eager, beetle-eating cuttie seems to agree with his opinion.

Long's CDC Euro Dun

- **Hook:** #18-22 fine wire scud hook
- **Thread:** 8/0, color to match body
- **Body:** Natural dubbing such as beaver dubbing, most often gray, brown, or olive
- **Wing:** CDC (cul de canard) feathers, tied Compara-dun style

I've mentioned previously in this book that the key to catching trout in Yellowstone National Park (or elsewhere for that matter) throughout the course of the season is sometimes showing the fish a fly pattern they don't often see. And that may be the Long's CDC Euro Dun's finest attribute. Matthew Long calls his fly a "Euro Dun" because it was inspired by fly patterns that his European clients brought with them to fish in the park. But, in another case of different anglers arriving at the same conclusion, the pattern is very similar to Charlie Craven's Mole Fly. The Euro Dun is tied similar to a CDC Compara-dun or Sparkle Dun, but without the split Microfibbet tail or Zelon trailing shuck, which these flies include.

When many anglers imagine fishing Yellowstone before their first visit, they often picture big trout rising naively to large foam flies. There's a reason they think this way: A lot of the park's trout are caught on big flies, particularly earlier in the season when the rivers are full of water and the fish haven't begun to respond to heavy angling pressure.

Matthew Long developed his CDC Euro Dun after guiding European clients that were using similar flies. Many anglers traveling to Yellowstone imagine that the fish will always eat large flies. But trout are trout, no matter where in the world they swim, and they sometimes become selective to eating small flies.

But there's another reason why many of the park's anglers seldom use tiny dry flies. A lot of anglers struggle to fish small dry flies—they are often difficult to see on the water (though Matthew says his fly is more visible than you might think), and the small gap between the hook's shank and point can make it difficult to hook fish. This is particularly true with large trout that have rigid mouths and is magnified by the slow manner in which cutthroat trout usually rise. It's vital to pause before setting the hook, particularly with a small fly, so the fish has a chance to close its mouth.

But as the water levels drop and trout become more nervous and selective, a large fly pattern can sometimes repel rather than attract them. That's when Matthew fishes his Euro Dun. "I fish these flies in the park because most other people don't fish this stuff," he told me. "But I'll even fish it as a single fly while floating the Yellowstone River [outside the park's boundaries]. My Euro Dun is more typically a spring creek pattern, and most anglers don't fish small, sparse flies like these in freestone streams. It's a 6X fly."

Matthew likes the pattern with a gray body for Blue-Winged Olives and a brown body for PMDs (Pale Morning Duns). I asked him why

Ruthann Weamer shows that big Yellowstone trout can sometimes be caught on small flies, particularly in the smooth water near the eroded bank in this photo.

he prefers to use a brown-bodied fly to imitate mayflies that are usually shades of yellow. He said, "I'm not really trying to imitate the dun [after a mayfly emerges from a nymph but before it transforms into a sexually mature adult spinner]. This fly looks like an emerger, like a captive dun." So Matthew is really using this fly to imitate PMDs that are just rising to the surface, still in their nymphal bodies, or at the early stages of escaping their nymphal shucks. This tiny dry fly is really being eaten as a floating nymph.

Fishing Techniques

Matthew always fishes his Euro Dun as a stand-alone dry fly, never in tandem with other flies. I asked him why he doesn't drop it off a larger dry fly to make it more visible. He said, "Two dry flies are floating in two different current streams, so neither fly floats at the actual flow [speed] of the water. I fish the flies at a downstream angle to rising fish. I use a reach cast and try to pile up my tippet and then shake a little line [extending a drift by wiggling the rod tip to release line] to get a longer drift." Matthew continued, "A lot of anglers struggle to fish down and across, but it's really important with this fly." He doesn't use this pattern throughout the season. "It's the perfect fly for fussy trout. I usually start fishing it when the drakes start to taper off, midsummer through fall."

As I mentioned, it can be difficult to get hook sets when you're fishing tiny flies (size 20 and smaller) like Long's Euro Dun. Make sure you're using the sharpest hooks you can find. Some anglers will even bend the hook point slightly out of line from the hook shank to help the fly stick into the tough parts of a trout's mouth, though this isn't as big a concern with Matthew's pattern because the extra hook gap that is created by using a fine wire scud hook helps facilitate better hook sets.

Shakey Beeley

- **Hook:** #8-12 (#10 is the most popular) Umpqua U204, Dai Riki 280, or TMC 2312
- **Thread:** Brown 6/0
- **Flash (underwing):** Pearl or hot orange Krystal Flash
- **Tail:** Tan wood duck or mallard flank
- **Abdomen:** Amber Hareline Super Fine
- **Rib:** Brown 3/0 UNI-Thread or UNI-Stretch
- **Thorax:** Orange ostrich herl
- **Hackle:** Natural Hungarian partridge

Bucky McCormick is a terrific fly tier who's been in the fly-fishing industry a long time. He is originally from Buffalo, New York, but moved to West Yellowstone seventeen years ago and began working at Blue Ribbon Flies. Winters in West Yellowstone are long and cold, and finding employment that time of year can be difficult. Bucky thought he'd try to become a park snowcoach driver when the fishing business slowed down, but he arrived too late in the season to secure the job. So when Blue Ribbon Flies offered him year-round employment, he stayed. He's been there ever since. Today he's the manager of one of West Yellowstone's most important fly shops, where some of our sport's most iconic fly patterns have been developed. I met with Bucky to discuss flies for this book, and he suggested I include the Shakey Beeley.

The Shakey Beeley was first introduced by Blue Ribbon Flies in 2002. Nick Nicklas, another famed fly tier who was originally from Pennsylvania, initially tied the fly to imitate Eastern March Browns. But today, the fly

The Shakey Beeley was created by well-known Blue Ribbon Flies guide and fly pattern designer Nick Nicklas. Sadly, Mr. Nicklas passed away in 2014, but he should be remembered every time an angler ties one of his terrific fly imitations to their leader.

is often used to imitate caddis. Mr. Nicklas added some Krystal Flash to the pattern after he moved to Montana, and created one of the park's most productive wet flies. He added the flash to get the attention of the lake-run brown trout, which ascend the Madison in the fall. "The fly is still the shop's number one wet fly," Bucky said. "I fish it all year long, but the browns like it best. I catch rainbow trout with it too. But there's just something about it that the browns love."

Nicklas named the Shakey Beeley after a seasonal Yellowstone National Park ranger whose hands shook as he stood, day after day, fishing in the Madison. He was there so often that there's also a riffle in the river, near the state line (border between the park and Montana), that locals call the Shakey Beeley.

I would have loved to talk with Mr. Nicklas about his ideas on fly design; his passing in 2014 assured that could not happen. But Bucky sent me a link to a Blue Ribbon Flies video of Nick tying the Shakey Beeley, which allowed me to glean some of the fly creator's thoughts, like why he included a tail for a caddis imitation when real caddis do not have tails. "They [caddis] always have legs, antennas, shucks, something hanging out the

Nick Nicklas added flash to the Shakey Beeley wet fly for catching fall-run brown trout that ascend the Madison River each year. Here the author shows a beautiful, midsized, fall-run brown trout from the Madison. (photo John Campbell)

back, and this is a modified March Brown soft hackle, so I just kind of left the tail in place," explained Nicklas in the video.

Soft hackles and wet flies are often forgotten tools for catching the park's trout, in spite of the fact that most of Yellowstone's earliest fly fishers were using them. Today, there is a small subset of dedicated wet-fly fishers throughout the United States, but their numbers are fewer than those anglers who spend most of their time fishing dry flies, nymphs, and streamers. This can be an advantage for any angler willing to delve into these effective flies and the techniques for using them—things that Yellowstone's trout don't always see.

Fishing Techniques

Versatility is perhaps the Shakey Beeley's (and all other wet flies') finest attribute: You can fish it however you like. Many anglers think of only traditional wet-fly methods for employing these types of patterns: Cast two wet flies (or three if you're outside the park), tied in tandem, either quartering downstream or initially upstream to allow them time to sink. Then force the flies to rise from deeper water by holding your line tight as they drag below you. Allow the flies to dangle in the current for a time, twitching beneath the surface like emergers. Strip them back to you, take a step downstream, and begin the process again.

But I've had success by dusting wet flies with floatant to make them briefly float for picky fish that are eating dry flies. You can also cast wets towards in-stream structure or the banks and strip them back to you like streamers. Sometimes it's effective to drop a wet fly off of the bend of a heavy nymph to get it to the stream bottom and then fish both flies on a dead drift as you would with two standard nymphs. I'm usually fishing wets with a 9-foot 4X leader if I'm using them only subsurface, but I'll go to 5X if I'm trying to deceive a particularly wary trout into eating one as a dry fly.

- **Hook:** #14-18 Dai Riki 135
- **Thread:** Brown, olive, pearl, or red 6/0
- **Bead:** Gold ⁷⁄₆₄-inch for #14, ³⁄₃₂-inch for #16, ⁵⁄₆₄-inch for #18
- **Body:** Brown, olive, pearl, or red 6/0
- **Rib:** Gold UTC wire (small)
- **Wing:** Deer hair

Three Dollar Dip

When I asked Blue Ribbon Flies' Bucky McCormick which patterns he thought I should include in this book, he said, "The Three Dollar Dip is a really good one." The Three Dollar Dip is another great fly pattern that came from the vise of Nick Nicklas. The fly is named after the famous Three Dollar Bridge access on the Madison River outside of Yellowstone National Park, but Bucky says it's also one of the best flies to catch fish inside the park. According to Bucky, "That color [brown] works especially well on the Madison [in and out of the park]. It must look a lot like the Madison's midge and caddis larvae."

Blue Ribbon Flies first introduced the Three Dollar Dip's bead-head version, now the most popular version, in 2006, but they were carrying a non-bead-head version a long time before that. The fly descended from another great pattern, the Serendipity, a midge larva imitation that has a body formed by twisting and then wrapping Zelon. Blue Ribbon Flies (along with John Betts) bought the world's entire supply of Zelon when the DuPont

The Three Dollar Dip, another of the great fly creations from the vise of Nick Nicklas, was named for the Three Dollar Bridge access on the Madison River outside the park. But Madison River fish inside the park (as well as fish most everywhere else) eat this fly too.

company discontinued its use as a material to make carpet. Craig Mathews (the former owner of Blue Ribbon Flies) quickly saw its value as a fly-tying material and added it to many flies, including the world-renowned X Caddis and Sparkle Dun.

Bucky told me that the shop still has some of that original material left. He said, "We have a few years supply remaining. The straight [there are two versions: straight and crinkled] will be gone first." But he also added that when it's gone, "it won't be that big of a deal these days. There are lots of similar options available to fly tiers today." But when it first appeared on the fly-fishing scene, it was a game changer.

Bucky said that in the '80s, "everyone was fishing big flies." So when the Serendipity and Three Dollar Dip came along, they were very effective. Bucky wanted to create an even slimmer version of the fly, so he designed his Montana Bullet. Bucky's fly, a new listing for Blue Ribbon Flies in 2020, takes the best elements from Perdigon nymphs, combined with Nicklas's Three Dollar Dip, to make a quick-sinking fly that works well in the park, and everywhere else trout live.

The Three Dollar Dip has a small tuft of deer hair to represent an emerging wing. But Bucky says that unlike many fly patterns where using the best hair you can find really makes or breaks a pattern, this isn't the case with the Three Dollar Dip. "Use the crummiest hair you have," he told me. "Don't waste your good hair on this fly." That's because the deer hair doesn't need to float. This pattern is designed to sink, to be fished like a nymph. The hair is only there as a trigger (something that convinces a fish that it's food) for the fly. Blue Ribbon Flies even sells patches of this cheap hair, specifically for tying the fly.

Bucky sent me an email discussing the Three Dollar Dip and the colors in which they tie and fish it: "As is always the case at Blue Ribbon Flies, we've experimented with every possible combination of this deadly design. The following colors are the best we've seen: brown, olive, pearl, and red. But brown, the original, is still the best color."

Fishing Techniques

I like to show fish options, so I nearly always fish two nymphs if I'm fishing with an indicator. The Three Dollar Dip is a good fly to trail behind a larger, or more heavily weighted, pattern that attracts the fish's attention. I fish the Three Dollar Dip behind a Pat's Rubber Legs or a Perdigon, and the fish often choose the smaller fly. But there are times, particularly when the water is low, that I opt for fishing two Three Dollar Dips. I usually employ two different colors when I do this, so a pearl one with a brown one, or any other contrasting version. But if the fish begin to eat one color more than the other, I often fish two identical Dips at the same time. You can cover more water, at varying depths, by doing this.

Bucky McCormick's Montana Bullet was designed to be an even simpler, quick-sinking cross between a Three Dollar Dip and a Perdigon.

- **Hook:** #14-20 competition hook or competition jig hook such as the Hanak H 480 BL Jig Wave, or heavy wire scud hook for more-traditional Zebra Midges
- **Bead:** Silver, gold, or copper
- **Thread:** 8/0, color to match body
- **Body:** Red, black, olive, brown, or gray 8/0
- **Wire:** Silver, gold, or copper (small)

Competition Zebra Midge

The Zebra Midge was invented by Ted Welling, a fly-fishing guide in Lees Ferry, Arizona. This simple fly, formed with four components—hook, thread, bead, wire—was intended to imitate a midge pupa, but it also looks a lot like a midge larva. I often fish this fly with a red body to look like the famed "Blood Worm" midge larva. When I'm fishing the red Zebra Midge in the fall, in streams where brown and brook trout spawn, friends often chide me that any fish I catch with it must have taken it for an egg pattern. Maybe

they do. Whatever the fish "think" about the Zebra Midge, I only know it's feelings of love.

The Zebra Midge is not a pattern that's particularly associated with Yellowstone National Park, but it can be very effective there. Most trout waters contain midge populations, though they are often associated with spring creeks and stillwater fisheries. Yellowstone is not famous for trout-filled spring creeks (most of the park's springs are hot springs, not ideal for trout that prefer water temperatures from 55 to 65 degrees). But the park does have a

This Competition Zebra Midge, tied on a park-ready barbless jig hook, is a great option to suspend beneath a terrestrial dry fly during late summer and fall low-water periods. Fish may even believe the fly to be an egg pattern when it's tied with a red body. Competition Zebra Midges with black, olive, red, and brown bodies are all effective.

lot of flat river pools, and ponds and lakes where anglers fish for trout, and nearly all of them have midges.

The original Zebra Midge was tied on a heavy wire scud hook with a brass bead. Most of the flies were tied small, with a size 18 being as big as most anglers used (though you would occasionally see them in size 16 and larger). My friend, the famed Pennsylvania fly fisherman Charlie Meck, created a Zebra Midge variation that he called the Almost Nothing, because it was. Charlie decided that the fly didn't need a thread body at all—just a bead, hook, and wire rib—because the shiny bronze hook looked enough like a midge larva's body for the fish to eat it. And they did.

Today's competition anglers, who are prohibited from using weight on their leaders, have developed many creative ways to ensure their flies descend to the stream bottom as quickly as possible. This includes the use of heavy tungsten beads and jig-head hooks. The Competition Zebra Midge that I'm featuring here is just a standard Zebra tied on a barbless competition-style jig hook. Not only does this fly sink quickly, getting into the trout's feeding zone faster than a traditional Zebra Midge, but its bead and hook also come ready to follow Yellowstone fishing rules: no lead, barbless hook.

Fishing Techniques

Most anglers fish a Zebra Midge by using it as the sunken fly in a dry-dropper tandem, tied to the bend of the dry fly's hook. Even the heaviest Competition Zebra doesn't weigh enough to be a burden on most standard dry flies' ability to float. And just like any other dry-dropper rig, the dry fly becomes a de facto strike indicator, but one with a hook in it. If the dry fly stops, hesitates, or sinks, you lift the rod tip assuming a trout has taken the Zebra Midge. Without a doubt, tandem-rig fly

fishing is the most effective way to fish for trout. I've also had success in the park by fishing a Competition Zebra Midge dropped off the bend of a larger, fast-sinking nymph such as the Perdigon. Doing this keeps the Zebra near the river bottom, where it is almost certainly perceived to be a midge or small caddis larva, rather than an emerger.

I generally don't fish Zebra Midges in heavy, fast-moving water. The flies just don't sink quickly enough, and they generally get ripped through the current before the fish have a chance to react to a tiny fly. The Zebra Midge tandem works best when you're fishing the braided water below a riffle before it slows further into a pool or in the pool itself, because that's where many midges emerge. Midge hatches can be found at any time during the park's fishing season. They can produce incredible numbers of insects, and this creates the reason wild trout feed on them: If there were only a few, the fish wouldn't be able to recover enough calories as they feed to make it beneficial for their survival.

The dying, straw-colored grass behind this rainbow trout that ate a red Competition Zebra Midge is an indicator that fall has arrived in Yellowstone, and that's when I prefer to fish these flies.

Purple Haze

- **Hook:** #12-18 standard dry-fly hook
- **Thread:** Purple 8/0
- **Tail:** Moose body hair (elk or deer body hair may be substituted)
- **Body:** Purple Super Floss, Flexi Floss, or other synthetic material
- **Parachute post:** White polypropylene yarn or calf body hair
- **Hackle:** Brown and grizzly mixed

The Purple Haze, invented by Montana fly-fishing guide Andy Carlson, is an attractor dry-fly pattern: one intended not to imitate anything found in nature, but rather to look enough like food to inspire trout to eat it. In the twenty years I spent managing three eastern US fly shops with large dry-fly selections, I didn't sell a single Purple Haze because we didn't carry them. Most eastern attractor dries are more muted in appearance, often tied with natural materials and colors more closely aligned with those found on real insects. But in the western United States, attractor flies tend to range from bright to downright gaudy, with flashy, synthetic materials and a wide range of colors. Around Yellowstone National Park, it may be impossible to find a fly shop that doesn't stock Purple Hazes.

I view the Purple Haze as a western version of the more subtle and less buoyant Parachute Adams, which is tied with hackle fibers for its tail. The Purple Haze uses air-pocketed body hair from a moose or elk for its tail, creating a slightly bulkier appearance but greatly aiding floatation. The Purple Haze's body is most often composed of a synthetic purple

Though the Purple Haze is similar to the Parachute Adams, the fly's deer hair tail and its purple-colored body are important differences that help make this attractor dry fly one of the most effective in the park.

material, often of a flashy, reflective nature that grabs the fish's attention. It's the definition of an attractor fly pattern. Most shops also carry a yellow version of the fly, aptly called the Yellow Haze.

Both of these flies are tied in the "parachute" style where a rooster hackle feather, taken from birds raised primarily to grow fly-tying feathers, is wound around a post, often made from some type of hair or synthetic yarn. The post allows the hackle to be wound parallel to the hook shank, and this is important. Many fly-fishing authors (particularly the legendary Pennsylvania hatch-master Vincent Marinaro) have written about the importance of the circular light pattern that's formed when an aquatic insect stands on the water and its feet create little dimples in the water's surface film. This light pattern is another triggering mechanism that encourages a fish to eat it.

The Purple Haze, as it was originally designed, had a calf body hair wing post. But I prefer to use synthetic yarn for the post, which absorbs floatant well and is a little more visible for the angler, as well as being easier to tie. The yarn also compresses tighter than calf tail, helping to control the bulk created in the fly's body when wrapping over the post's butts.

Fishing Techniques

Attractor dry-fly patterns are generally fished drag-free after being cast to likely trout-holding areas: edges of deeper water, along rocks and boulders or any other in-stream structure, and in riffles. But Yellowstone National Park anglers will sometimes use both Purple and Yellow Hazes during actual mayfly emergences. Just mimic the shade of the insect that's hatching to decide which one to use: For dark-colored mayflies, go with the Purple Haze. Anything on the lighter side (especially during Pale Morning Dun hatches), go with the Yellow Haze. In my experience, trout are much less concerned with imitating the exact color of an insect, but fly pattern size and color shade can be very important. For example, you usually don't want to be fishing a big, dark-colored fly when the fish are eating small, light-colored ones.

Parachute-style flies like the Purple and Yellow Hazes work best when they are fished in moderate- to smooth-flowing waters. Because their parallel-wound hackles keep their bodies close to the surface, they're more likely to absorb the water, making them less buoyant than flies tied with hackles wound perpendicular to their hook shanks such as Wulff-style flies (see the Rubber Leg Royal Wulff chapter). The incorporation of deer hair in its tail, rather than the chicken hackle fibers used in many eastern parachute fly designs, does aid the Purple Haze's ability to remain floating, but there are still-better options for fishing turbulent water. The flush way in which they sit on the water also makes parachute-style flies more difficult to see in areas of heavy current. I generally fish the Hazes (both Purple and Yellow) with a 9-foot leader and 5X tippet.

Adams, Standard and Parachute

- **Hook:** #10-20 standard dry-fly hook
- **Thread:** Black 8/0
- **Tail:** Mixed brown and grizzly hackle fibers
- **Body:** Gray beaver dubbing
- **Wing post (parachute):** Calf body hair or polypropylene yarn, white or fluorescent-colored to aid visibility
- **Hackle:** Mixed brown and grizzly

The Adams was invented by Michigan's Leonard Halladay in the early 1920s. His fly, which was tied a little differently than the pattern that has become the standard today, is probably the most commonly fished dry fly throughout North America. Its use in Yellowstone National Park began almost as soon as fly-fishing tourists began fishing dry flies there. In his book *Remembrances of Rivers Past* (Macmillan, 1972), legendary fly fisherman Ernest (Ernie) Schwiebert mentions the Adams as a good fly to use for fishing the park's Firehole River. And the fly still excels there, just as it does in nearly all of Yellowstone's trout waters.

The modern Adams is most commonly used in two iterations, the standard style and the parachute style, though there are other versions as well. A standard Adams is tied with a mix of brown and grizzly hackles that are wrapped perpendicular (wrapped around) the hook shank with upright, divided grizzly hen hackle wings. Tying the hackle this way makes the fly sit higher on the water's surface,

The standard Adams is one of the most commonly fished attractor dry flies in the United States. The fly isn't a perfect match for any exact aquatic insect, but it looks like several of them. Perhaps it works so well just because it looks like a bug.

adding visibility for the angler and increasing the pattern's buoyancy, since its body has less contact with the water than when tied parachute style.

The Parachute Adams's hackles are also a mix of brown and grizzly rooster hackles, but they are formed parallel to the hook shank by wrapping them around a parachute post, just like the Purple Haze. Both versions work very well for most applications, but the Parachute Adams is better suited for use in flat water and for imitating emerging insects. The standard Adams excels when fished in riffles and for mimicking mayflies that quickly flee from the water immediately after exiting their nymphal shuck.

I always carry both styles in my park fly boxes. But if I were forced to choose only one to use throughout the season, it would be the Parachute Adams. Its flush-riding posture makes it appear more helpless, like a mayfly emerger or a spinner, and less likely to flee from a rising trout. Trout actively search for helpless insects because they provide easy meals. Although, as stated earlier, the Adams is not intended to imitate an exact insect, it is a very good imitation of gray-colored *Callibaetis* mayflies, which are most commonly found in stillwaters (ponds and lakes), and Gray Drakes, which may be found in waters throughout the park.

Fishing Techniques

Perhaps the reason the Adams is used so often by anglers is that it's a very versatile pattern. In addition to using the pattern to imitate gray-colored flies, it's also a passable imitation for olive mayflies (Western Green Drakes, Blue-Winged Olives) and even creamy brown ones such as Brown Drakes. The park's trout are generally not inclined to refuse a dry fly simply because it doesn't perfectly match the color of the naturals it's been eating. I've

found that fly pattern size and silhouette, and the way in which the fly is presented (drag-free, twitched), is much more important than matching an exact color.

The beauty of the Adams is that you don't have to wait until you see insects emerging and trout rising to fish the fly. It is very effective when used as a searching pattern while you're blind casting. I've caught several memorable trout from the park's Slough Creek while dropping a Parachute Adams off the back of a Chubby in a double dry-fly tandem rig.

This technique (using a dry-fly tandem with a smaller pattern trailing from a larger Chubby) also works well with the similar-looking Purple Haze. But trout sometimes want flies to appear more muted, and the Adams's natural gray-colored dubbed body can occasionally be a better option than the brighter, flashier Purple Haze's body. Though the inverse is also sometimes true. The best way to know for sure which fly the fish will want is to fish both patterns (Parachute Adams and Purple Haze) simultaneously in a dry-fly tandem rig. Drop one of them off the bend of the other's hook, and let the park's trout tell you which one they prefer.

This big rainbow ate a Parachute Adams trailed behind a Chubby on Slough Creek. Most of the time I'm fishing an Adams, I prefer the parachute version.

- **Hook:** #10-16 1XL dry-fly hook
- **Thread:** 6/0, color to match body
- **Tail:** Elk body hair
- **Back and wing:** Elk body hair pulled over hook shank from tail to form wing
- **Underbody:** Beaver or synthetic dubbing. Colors can be whatever you want them to be, but yellow, red, and green are probably the most common.
- **Hackle:** Various colors to match body, or often a buggy-looking mix of brown and grizzly

Humpy
(aka Goofus Bug)

The Humpy, along with the much more entertainingly named Goofus Bug (same fly, two different names), is one of those fly patterns that is found in most western fly anglers' boxes, though a lot of eastern fly fishers use it too. Bruce Staples and Bob Jacklin, in their terrific book about the history of West Yellowstone's fly-fishing industry, *Fly Fishing West Yellowstone: A History and Guide* (Stackpole, 2021), give credit for the pattern's popularity to the Pat Barnes Fly Shop, specifically Sigrid Barnes, who the authors claim tied the fly as her "signature" pattern. Staples and Jacklin also state that Barnes credited Keith Kenyon for originating the fly for use on the Firehole River.

The book reports that the name Goofus Bug came from the Barnes duo being asked about that "goofy deer hair fly" after a story about it was published in a fishing magazine. But in Wyoming, for some reason, it was simultaneously known as the Humpy. Most anglers today call the fly a Humpy—that's the name you'll see attached to the bins in most

The Humpy, also known as the Goofus Bug, is ideally suited for blind casting in turbulent waters. The fly is constructed with a significant amount of elk hair in relation to its size, and this makes it very buoyant and easy for anglers to see on the water.

fly shops. And though I'm still hoping for a "Goofus Bug" resurgence, I'll use its more common moniker here.

Humpies generally work best in turbulent rivers and creeks where a fly's buoyancy and visibility (for the angler) are of greater importance than its ability to subtly match a specific aquatic insect—the flies don't really look like anything you'd find hatching in trout water. But the fish don't seem to mind. Humpies are highly visible, and they float so well because of the unique way in which they are tied: Extra-long strands of air-pocket-filled deer, or elk, body hair are tied along the hook shank with their stacked tips extending past the fly's tail. The butts are then covered with thread and dubbing along the hook shank. To form the wing, the hair is then pulled back over the top of the fly's underbody, towards the hook eye, to form a "humped" back and create a divided wing. Hackle is added around the wing, and the fly is now complete.

Using this much deer hair, combined with hackle, on relatively small dry-fly hooks (most are tied from size 10 to 16) keeps the flies floating high in the roughest of waters but

This angler is fishing ideal Humpy water. The heavy current will push a fly pattern downstream very quickly, giving the fish less time to decide to eat it. A dry fly needs to be buoyant and visible to the angler to be effective here. The Humpy checks both of those boxes.

also makes them appear bulky. So you generally don't want to give the fish a good look at them by fishing Humpies in slow, glassy-clear pools. Though you should never say "never" in fly fishing, and I'm sure as soon as some anglers read this they'll say, "I've caught trout in slow water with Humpies!" I have too, so it's definitely possible. But these flies really excel in rough, fast water much more so than calm, placid flows.

If you want to show the trout an especially large morsel, particularly if you're fishing exceptionally turbulent, rapid water, then you can tie two Humpies onto one extra-long-shanked streamer or nymph hook. This contraption is called a Double Humpy and is generally best fished in the heaviest water in the park's largest rivers.

Fishing Techniques
I usually fish Humpies in braided water, riffles, and calmer areas within rapids along in-stream structure such as large boulders or downed trees, but the flies work best anywhere there's enough slack current, bordered by moving water, to contain a trout. So look for drop-offs, where shallow water meets deep water (most often greenish in color), too.

I generally begin fishing Humpies on a dead drift, without movement, but twitching them in front of an obvious trout-holding lie can also work well. Sometimes, dragging the fly along the surface to mimic a struggling insect can illicit explosive strikes. Make sure you're employing the heaviest tippet (3X or even heavier) that the trout will accept if you're going to use the flies this way.

I've also had success intentionally plopping Humpies on the surface like you might do with a terrestrial pattern, imitating a creature that has flown or fallen into the water. Just don't slap the fly so aggressively that your fly line slams the water, scaring the trout.

Woolly Worm

- **Hook:** #8-14 4XL nymph or streamer hook
- **Thread:** Black 3/0
- **Tail:** Tuft of red wool yarn
- **Body:** Black chenille
- **Ribbing:** Silver flat or oval tinsel
- **Hackle:** Grizzly neck or saddle, tied palmered over the body

The Woolly Worm is one of the oldest fly patterns in this book. It's one of the first flies I learned to tie, and it's so ubiquitous that you can usually find it for sale any place that carries a basic fly selection, from hardware stores and gas stations to Walmart, though it's less common in modern fly shops. But for all its longevity, many serious fly fishers no longer consider it an option for their fly boxes. That's a mistake, particularly if you're fishing in Yellowstone National Park.

According to West Yellowstone's Bob Jacklin, the Woolly Worm was "designed, tied, and popularized by Don Martinez in the 1930s through Don's Tackle Shop in West Yellowstone." Mr. Jacklin goes on to say, "Don modestly claimed not to have invented the Woolly Worm, but to have modified an old bass fly whose hackles were wrapped 'palmer style' [over the whole body]." He also states that Martinez was the person responsible for naming the fly. "It lasted as a real fish-catcher through the 1960s, when someone changed the fly, added a marabou tail, and changed the name to the Woolly Bugger."

The Woolly Worm is one of the oldest fly patterns in this book. At one time, it was a staple for Yellowstone National Park fly fishers. But it isn't as popular with today's anglers, though the fly still works as well as when it was first popularized nearly ninety years ago.

That person was Pennsylvania's Russ Blessing, who earned legendary status where I learned to fly fish because of his pattern. You can probably find a version of Blessing's Woolly Bugger in every fly shop in the United States (and around most of the world). I was told that Mr. Blessing invented his fly to imitate hellgrammites, the larval form of the dobsonfly, which are common in some Pennsylvania waters.

I don't know for certain whether or not Mr. Blessing was aware of the Woolly Worm when he tied his first Bugger, but due to the identical "Woolly" in each of their names, I would guess that he was. And though giving proper credit for things like fly pattern creation is extremely important for recognizing significant advancements in fly-fishing history, the trout don't really give a damn.

Small things matter in fly fishing, and a simple change that replaced a Woolly Worm's red tag with a Woolly Bugger's marabou tail made a huge difference. And the two patterns are often fished differently. It's uncommon to fish a Woolly Worm on the stream bottom like a nymph, which you can do with a Woolly Bugger. And it's uncommon (maybe never?) to fish a Woolly Bugger as a dry fly like you often do

Russ Blessing's Woolly Bugger (tied by Bruce Miller) is basically a Woolly Worm with a marabou tail. But the flies are designed to be fished differently, and they both belong in every Yellowstone National Park anglers' fly boxes.

with a Woolly Worm. As we fly fishers should probably know best, the devil is in the details. Fly-fishing mountains have been moved by the addition or subtraction of the little things.

Fishing Techniques

Though the Woolly Worm was designed to be fished either wet or dry, I tend to use it most often as a dry fly. The fly can be tied in any color combination of hackle and body materials, which makes it very versatile. But if you fish an area where caterpillars are commonly found, it's a fair guess that the Woolly Worm looks enough like one to be eaten as its imitation. A smaller Woolly Worm might suggest a caddisfly. And if you tie the fly with all-black materials, you could be imitating many types of terrestrial insects.

I generally begin fishing a Woolly Worm as a dry fly by blind casting it upstream and allowing it to float back to me with a dead drift. But it floats well enough, after being greased with floatant, that you can also intentionally "skitter" it (purposefully dragging it across the water's surface) to imitate an emerging caddis.

The Woolly Worm is also an effective wet-fly attractor pattern. To fish it wet, I begin by squeezing the fly underwater after I tie it to my 9-foot 3X leader (sometimes, if the water is particularly deep or swift-moving, I add a non-lead split shot to my leader approximately 6 inches above it). Then I usually cast it upstream, allowing it to sink while mending my fly line upstream as the fly drifts towards me. Once the fly drifts downstream from my position, I hold the line tight, forcing the Woolly Worm to swing towards the surface like an emerging insect.

I also occasionally fish a Woolly Worm like a small streamer, casting it towards a stream bank or in-stream structure and stripping it back to me with short, quick tugs on my fly line.

- **Hook:** #10-16 standard dry-fly hook
- **Thread:** Black 8/0
- **Body:** Peacock herl, divided in middle of hook shank by several turns of purple or red thread, floss, or synthetic dubbing
- **Tail:** Deer or elk body hair
- **Wing:** Most often tied with calf tail or body (to give a less kinky look) hair, but white polypropylene yarn can also be used.
- **Legs:** Medium brown MFC Sexi-Floss (small)
- **Hackle:** Dark coachman brown

Rubber Leg Royal Wulff

Did you know that Yellowstone National Park has a Royal Wulff season? Well, it's not official, but I often discuss it with my friends and guiding clients. It begins right about the time that most of the park's trout are tired of eating big, foam-bodied Chubbies and hoppers, and they begin refusing them, or often ignoring them altogether. This is when I start casting other things that maybe the fish haven't seen for a while. I realize that my fanciful "Royal Wulff season" could be construed as the entire fishing season in many of the park's smaller, more isolated and less pressured fisheries, which are often filled with gullible little brook or cutthroat trout, but I'm not talking about these streams. What I'm discussing takes place on the other waterways, the famous and often crowded ones that usually flow close to roads, creating easy angler access and the intense fly-fishing pressure that comes with it.

The Royal Wulff was invented by fly-fishing legend Lee Wulff to be a more buoyant attractor fly (one that doesn't imitate a specific insect), better suited to the often rough-and-tumble western trout fisheries. The flies

Western anglers seem to add rubber legs to any fly pattern they can. The legs look buggy and add movement that can trigger a trout to strike. I've caught some of my best Yellowstone National Park trout on the many variations of Wulff dry-fly patterns.

appear more substantial, fuller-dressed, than the refined, sparsely tied dries that emanated from the generally more placid streams in New York's Catskill Mountains region and the fabled Pennsylvania limestone fisheries. Wulffs are considered a tying style, so a fly tier can create versions for specific uses by changing materials or material colors: White Wulffs, AuSable Wulffs, Gray Wulffs, etc.

Pennsylvania fly-fishing legend Charlie Meck created his own Wulff-like pattern, the Patriot, by replacing the Royal Wulff's peacock herl body with one made from a synthetic material, smolt blue Krystal Flash. The Patriot's synthetic body makes the fly a little more durable and gives it an extra flash that would be impossible to create with natural materials.

One of the Royal Wulff alterations I like best for fishing in the park (it is also an effective addition to Charlie Meck's Patriot) is the incorporation of small, fine legs that make the flies appear a little buggier. The silicon legs used to tie them are very thin and malleable. They twitch and shudder with gentle breezes, or even the pull from the water's current, creating the appearance of life. It's generally a good idea to have a supply of Wulff variations, tied in multiple colors and sizes, with you in the park—you never know what might work on any given fishing day.

Fishing Techniques

Rubber Leg Wulffs and Patriots are not intended to be exact replicas of anything found in nature, so you won't find their natural counterparts hatching in park waters. This means that if you find trout rising to an explicit aquatic, or terrestrial, insect hatch, it's probably not a good time to try one when a more insect-imitating pattern is likely what the fish want. But when you're fishing faster water without obvious surface-feeding trout, particularly when flows are dwindling during late summer, Wulffs become a great option.

Their white calf tail, or body, hair wings make them visible, much of the time, though they can be more difficult to see if you're fishing them in whitewater-adjacent seams or white foam lines. Tiers sometimes form the wings from fluorescent yellow, pink, or other more visible colors to use in these areas.

I most often fish Wulffs by blind casting them to areas that are likely to hold a trout—deeper, calmer pockets of water either in or adjacent to fast-moving areas. I work my way upstream, casting my fly into the fast water, allowing the current to bring it back downstream to me as I strip in excess line to remove slack, preparing to set the hook by keeping the fly line between my index finger and the rod's cork handle. I usually fish Wulffs by themselves in the park on a 9-foot 4X or 5X leader, but they work very well in tandem with another less visible dry fly (perhaps a small black ant) or a bead-head nymph. Just keep your nymphs on the smaller side (generally size 14 and under, depending upon their weight) because, though they're buoyant by themselves, Wulffs aren't able to support much weight hanging beneath them and remain floating on the surface.

This Patriot (tied by Charlie Meck) is a Royal Wulff variation. Charlie got the idea to replace the Royal Wulff's peacock herl body with one made from smolt blue Krystal Flash after reading a study that found trout to be attracted to the color blue.

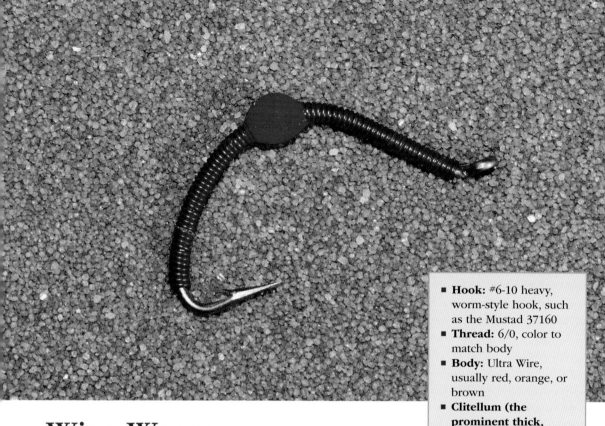

- **Hook:** #6-10 heavy, worm-style hook, such as the Mustad 37160
- **Thread:** 6/0, color to match body
- **Body:** Ultra Wire, usually red, orange, or brown
- **Clitellum (the prominent thick, unsegmented part of a worm):** Epoxy over thread or a bead, color to match body

Wire Worm

In a book where I've often focused on classic flies, which are beautifully tied, it feels a little like heresy to feature a worm pattern. And if you're a dry-fly purist, I have no doubt that you'll want to move quickly past this entry. But if you want to catch Yellowstone National Park's trout (or trout just about anywhere for that matter), give me a chance. A lot of fly-fishing "facts" get written once and then repeated throughout history in the myriad books and articles for which our sport is famous. But, occasionally, long-held fly-fishing

beliefs are simply that, akin more to myths that aren't necessarily provable with scientific methods, but rather passed down from one generation to the next with blind faith. And such is the belief that trout often eat worm patterns because terrestrial worms are washed into waterways after a rainstorm.

I'm not sure where this theory originated. Perhaps someone saw some worms slithering around their driveway after a significant rain event and decided that must be how they get into streams. I've read about this idea many

Worm patterns may not be the most glamorous flies for catching trout, but they are some of the most effective. Aquatic worms live in the substrate of most trout streams, and fish actively eat these calorie-dense foods.

times, and really didn't think much about it until I began stream sampling (not in the park, where it's not allowed), first out of curiosity and eventually for my own books and articles. Here's what I found: aquatic worms living, year-round, beneath the water just like mayfly, caddis, and stonefly nymphs in nearly every stream I sampled. I'm not arguing that it's impossible for terrestrial worms to get flushed into rivers and creeks, but isn't it much more likely that when waterways rise after storm events, worms already in them get churned up a little? The amount of stream bank erosion that must occur for land-dwelling worms to be flushed after rain, though possible, certainly isn't common.

Regardless of how worms get into Yellowstone National Park's waterways, as every child with a push-button bait-fishing outfit and a gob of nightcrawlers can attest, trout love them. And though there are several effective worms patterns used by today's anglers, my favorite is the Wire Worm. Perhaps the Wire Worm's greatest attribute, besides its often bright red, trout-attracting color, is that the fly sinks very well—nearly the entire pattern is formed from metal. This gives it weight, more so than what's found in most other worm fly patterns.

Everything on this fly, from its heavy wire hook to the metallic wire used to form its body, is made to help the fly sink to the stream bottom. And that's where you want to fish a Wire Worm: bouncing along the gravel and cobbles, like any other nymph pattern. Aquatic worms crawl along the stream bottom until they are dislodged. Then they generally hang, curved in posture, in the water's currents until they descend once again to the safety of streambed structure. They sometimes twitch and move as they try to rectify their position, and I've had some luck purposefully twitching my Wire Worms.

Fishing Techniques

I fish Wire Worms most often in tandem with another fast-sinking nymph like a Perdigon, attached to 3X or 4X tippet. I use the Wire Worm as the lead fly, tied to my leader, and the smaller nymph as the dropper. The Wire Worms I usually fish are either red or orange colored, and I really haven't had either color work better than the other. Purple, brown, white, and even black Wire Worms are also common.

Though Wire Worms catch trout throughout the year, I'm particularly fond of using them when the water level is a little higher than normal or when it's colored from sediment that's been stirred up after a heavy rain or snowmelt runoff. In somewhat of a contradiction, I also like to fish Wire Worms during autumn's low river flows with an egg pattern as a dropper. Yellowstone's trout, like trout everywhere, seem to be energized to feed heavily as diminishing light and colder temperatures provide a warning of the unstoppable march towards winter. This, combined with increased brown and brook trout aggression from spawning hormones, seems to make the fish more willing to attack gaudy patterns like the Wire Worm.

This beautiful Yellowstone National Park rainbow trout wasn't too proud to eat a Wire Worm. If the fish don't care about angler-inspired disdain for these types of flies, then why should the anglers? The most successful fly fishers give the trout what they want to eat.

- **Hook:** #12-16 egg hook or heavy wire scud hook
- **Thread:** 6/0, color to match predominant body color
- **Body:** Egg yarn or McFly Foam, Oregon cheese (my favorite color), pink, orange, blue, or other color of choice, with a smaller piece of red in the body's center

Egg Patterns

If you thought the Wire Worm entry was an affront to the purist fly fisherman, then you're really going to hate my recommendation for fishing egg patterns in the park. But our flies are supposed to imitate trout food, and if you're not fishing eggs in the fall before the whitefish, brookies, and brown trout spawn, then you're not really targeting what the trout want to eat. It's important to mention that all of the park's trout are wild. No one is coming with buckets of hatchery fish to replace the ones that anglers, other predators, fires, floods, and anchor ice kill. So we

need to protect them. This means it's highly unethical to try to catch any trout you might find actively spawning in the fall.

Yellowstone National Park's fishing season—opening after most cutthroats, rainbows, and cuttbows have spawned in the spring and closing before most whitefish and brown and brook trout spawn in the fall—ensures that anglers will leave most of the fish unhampered to finish their important species-preserving business. The primary reason that the park's fishing season doesn't open until late May is to protect the native, spawning cutthroat

Egg patterns, like worm patterns, are considered "junk flies" by some anglers. But our flies are supposed to imitate natural foods that trout eat, and just like they do with worms, trout eat eggs.

trout. But their eggs don't hatch immediately from the gravel, and you can still crush and destroy them if you walk through a redd that was made in the weeks previous to your fishing trip. So watch where you step. But, all that said, if trout are eating eggs, and you're not intentionally interfering with their love life by targeting them on their nests, then it's fair game. Not all trout spawn at the same time, so even if you see a few fish on active redds, some have probably already finished spawning, and others have yet to begin. Just don't target the ones still on the redds.

There are a lot of egg pattern iterations, but my favorite is a simple egg yarn (or McFly Foam) fly tied with a red dot in its center. This fly, popularized by Great Lakes steelheader Jeff Blood, is called the Blood Dot Egg. I'm not exactly sure why adding a small red dot to the egg's center makes the fly so much more effective than those without it. Perhaps the dot makes the fly look realistic, or the two-tone effect makes it more visible to the fish. Whatever it is, I always prefer egg patterns with a red dot to those without it.

There's an old fishing adage that goes, "If it ain't chartreuse, it ain't no use." While I don't prefer actual chartreuse-colored egg patterns—though I have caught fish on them from time to time—I always start with the color called Oregon cheese, which has a little hint of chartreuse color. But some park anglers I know prefer pink- or peach-colored flies. I use these colors too, on occasion, because just like with every other fly pattern, sometimes a color change can influence the trout to take one fly over another.

Fishing Techniques

Some natural eggs bounce across the stream bottom when they are released by a female trout into her redd. They are nearly weightless. That's why I prefer to use unweighted eggs, which are pulled to the stream bottom by a much heavier nymph such as a Perdigon. You're using two flies in this scenario, with the egg fished behind a heavy nymph, attached by a piece of tippet to the bend of its hook.

Fish the flies anywhere there's enough current to move them along the stream bottom, particularly in riffles and the braided water below them. You want to fish them without drag, because eggs can't move or swim. Strikes can be subtle when trout allow an egg pattern to float into their mouths. So any change in your indicator's behavior—even a slight pause or shudder—should cause you to lift your rod tip expecting a fish to be on the end of your line. I've had many guide clients, over the years, tell me that their flies bumped a rock when their indicator acted this way, but there's no way to know that unless you set the hook. Don't be one of those anglers. If it was a rock, just drop your rod tip and continue with the drift or recast. If it wasn't a rock, well, you missed that fish, so you need to cast again anyway.

This beautiful rainbow trout ate an egg pattern during an early fall fishing trip. You can fish egg imitations any time during the park's fishing season, but I find that they're most effective in the fall.

- **Hook:** #4-10 Tiemco 200R
- **Bead:** Black tungsten
- **Thread:** 6/0, color to match body
- **Body:** Synthetic dubbing, color to match wing
- **Collar:** Marabou, color to match wing
- **Wing/tail:** Pine squirrel strip, most often white, black, olive, tan, or brown

Big Sky Anglers' Barr's Bouface Leech

Leech-type streamers are very effective for catching trout. But calling these flies "leeches" is somewhat misleading. I've sampled the creatures living on stream bottoms of many rivers and creeks in both the eastern and western United States with a kick-net, and I've never found an all-white leech. Nearly all of streams I've sampled contain populations of leeches. Trout love to eat them, and they provide a great caloric source for the fish. But most leeches range in color from a light tan to black. The name "leech" has become synonymous with streamer patterns that are tied with soft materials that move in the water in a similar fashion to leeches. But that's probably all they have in common with real blood-suckers.

It's possible when you're fishing a brown or black leech streamer that trout believe it to be a leech, though most real leeches are also smaller than the flies we're fishing. But if you're using a white Bouface Leech, and the fish are eating it, they're most likely taking the fly as a baitfish imitation. Who cares what

I've never seen a white leech, so trout probably take this Barr's Bouface Leech, altered to make it more effective for fishing in the park by Big Sky Anglers' co-owner Jonathan Heames, as a baitfish imitation. The guys at Big Sky Anglers like to fish this fly with Spey rods for lake-run fish in the fall.

the fish believe they're eating? As long as it works, use it. And the Big Sky Anglers' version of John Barr's Bouface Leech works very well in Yellowstone National Park.

Joe Moore, co-owner of Big Sky Anglers fly shop in West Yellowstone, told me when we were discussing the Bouface Leech, "That thing works everywhere, but it's often a fall thing. Spey fishing [both single- and two-handed Spey rods (see page 107)] is really popular in our shop, and a lot of guys will swing the Bouface on a Spey [rod] for lake-run browns in the fall. But sometimes I'll also fish the Bouface on a standard fly rod with a floating line and a long leader, just jigging the fly [slowly raising and lowering the fly in the water by raising and lowering the rod tip] or by more common streamer techniques like casting the fly to the banks and just stripping it back."

The Bouface sold at Big Sky Anglers is a variation of the popular John Barr streamer pattern. "Ours is tied with a tungsten bead, so that it's legal to fish in Yellowstone National Park [remember, no lead in the park]," Moore told me. "And it also sinks like a rock. It was first tied by one of my business partners, Jonathan Heames, and it's a great pattern for stripping and swinging throughout Yellowstone. Our personal favorite is olive, but the white works pretty well too."

Fishing Techniques

Like Joe Moore mentioned, it's become popular to swing streamer and leech patterns with single- or two-handed Spey rods in the park. Anglers have developed multiple techniques for swinging flies, but here's how I normally do it: Cast your fly upstream, often towards a stream bank or in-stream structure. Allow the fly to sink by mending your line. Once the fly sinks to your desired depth (some anglers try to control their fly's depth by counting the seconds it sinks before they allow it to swing),

remove the slack from your line by stripping just enough of it back to you that it becomes tight and you are now in full contact with the fly. Follow the fly with your rod's tip, and as it begins to float past you, hold the line to allow the fly to drag. Continue to hold the line tight, allowing the fly to swing through the current, towards the surface, until it is now dangling directly below you. I sometimes tug on the line a couple times at this point, jigging the fly, but then I strip it back to me, take a step or two downstream, recast, and begin the process again.

You don't have to swing the Bouface for it to be effective for catching trout. I most often cast this fly to in-stream structure or stream banks, and simply strip it back to me. But if the fish are following your fly back to you without eating it, you need to either change how fast you're stripping (often strip more quickly to invoke a predatory response), strip more erratically to make the fly look wounded, or change the fly's color or size—maybe even switch patterns altogether.

Streamers of all types, including the Bouface Leech, are good options for fishing Yellowstone's fall season as large brown trout become aggressive before their spawn. On any given day, one color can produce better than another. I always carry white, black, yellow, and olive streamers when I plan to fish them. (photo Ruthann Weamer)

- **Hook:** #10-14 2XL
  nymph hook
- **Bead:** Copper
- **Thread:** Brown 8/0
- **Tail:** Brown partridge
  feather fibers
- **Body:** Dark gray hare's
  ear dubbing
- **Rib:** Heavy-gauge
  copper wire
- **Legs:** Brown partridge
  feather fibers

Minch's Bead, Hare, and Copper

The Parks' Fly Shop website, in describing the Minch's Bead, Hare, and Copper, says, "This is not a Hare's Ear [nymph], and we get annoyed when people say it is. This is what we use instead of a Hare's Ear." Even in person, Richard Parks, the Gardiner, Montana, fly shop's owner, becomes animated at the thought that someone might not realize the important differences between this fly and the world-renowned Hare's Ear. "It [the Bead, Hare, and Copper] is one hell of a great nymph. Some people look at it and just say,

'Oh, that's a Hare's Ear Nymph,' but it's different," Parks exclaimed as we spoke in his shop. It's the implementation of buggy-looking partridge feather fibers, the heavy-gauge copper wire rib, and a somewhat flattened body that Parks believes makes the fly more effective than the run-of-the-mill Hare's Ear.

In a telephone conversation, Matt Minch, the fly's creator, told me that he developed the pattern sometime in the early '90s after one of his trips to New Zealand—he's gone fishing there seventeen times so far. "I got the idea

Small changes can produce big results when it comes to altering fly patterns. Though this Minch's Bead, Hare, and Copper looks similar to a Hare's Ear Nymph, the two patterns are different, and that matters to the trout.

from a similar fly that's well known in New Zealand," he said. "After a while of fishing it in Yellowstone, I began to wonder why the hell I was still fishing a Hare's Ear when this fly was so much more effective. I never tied on a Hare's Ear again."

Richard Parks claims that the Bead, Hare, and Copper is usually his shop's single most effective fly for fall-run brown trout. Large brown trout ascend many of Yellowstone National Park's streams from lakes, and primary rivers, to spawn in the fall, creating opportunities to catch much larger than normal specimens. But the opportunities to target these pre-spawn fish (it's considered unethical to try to catch wild trout that are actively engaged in spawning) are fleeting, as Yellowstone's fishing season draws to a close in early November and inclement weather, including travel-inhibiting snow, can appear at any time. This time of year (late September through the season's closure) also brings greater threats

The guys at Parks' Fly Shop like to use the Bead, Hare, and Copper in the fall for lake-run and pre-spawn brown trout when most anglers are throwing large, gaudy patterns at the fish. Ruthann Weamer demonstrates that sometimes a little fly pattern can produce big results.

from the grizzlies and, to a much lesser degree, black bears as the large bruins enter a period known as hyperphagia, where they aggressively eat anything they can to prepare for their long winter slumber.

But why would aggressive, pre-spawn trout that are usually chasing streamers or eating bright egg patterns during the fall want to eat a bland-looking Bead, Hare, and Copper? The Parks' Fly Shop website has a colorful thought about that: "It's much smaller than what most people use for these fish, but that means it's like a fly buzzing around the fish's head, rather than a snarling dog getting in the fish's face. You don't think twice about swatting a fly, do you?" Lots of Yellowstone's trout have swatted this fly over the years.

Fishing Techniques

The Bead, Hare, and Copper works well either as a single fly or in a two-fly nymph rig, generally fished with a 9-foot leader and 4X tippet. Fish the flies drag-free, occasionally bouncing them against the stream bottom.

Earlier in the season, I use the Bead, Hare, and Copper as a dropper in tandem with a large Rubber Legs. I always fish two nymphs at a time, most often two dissimilar nymphs: a small one with a large one; a brightly colored pattern with a more muted fly; a pattern that incorporates synthetic, flashy materials in its construction with one made from earth-toned natural materials; or a bead-head fly with a fly tied without a bead.

When fishing the Bead, Hare, and Copper in the fall for pre-spawn brown trout, I usually like to drop it off the bend of a large, bright fly such as a red Wire Worm. It seems like the brighter-colored fly captures the trout's attention, but then they see and eat the Bead, Hare, and Copper. I also sometimes fish the Bead, Hare, and Copper as the lead fly, with an egg imitation dropper.

Spruce Fly

- **Hook:** #4-8 Mustad 79580 or equivalent long-shank streamer hook
- **Thread:** Black 6/0
- **Tail:** Small clump of peacock swords
- **Abdomen:** Red floss
- **Thorax:** Peacock herl
- **Rib:** Gold or silver wire
- **Wing:** Two badger hackles
- **Hackle:** Badger, tied as a collar

I was in West Yellowstone's Big Sky Anglers fly shop when one of their employees, Michael Delfino, asked if he could help me. I told him I was writing a book about the favorite flies for Yellowstone National Park, and he spent some time with me at the fly bins, telling me about what he and the shop's guides like to fish. But then he got a gleam in his eyes and said, "I have a fly for you," and he disappeared into a back room. When Michael reappeared he was holding a fly I knew, but one that I hadn't seen in a long time. It was

a Spruce Fly. Michael told me that the Spruce Fly has been responsible for some terrific fall days on the Madison River in the park, when the big brown trout are ascending to spawn. He said, in true Yogi Berra fashion, "It's one of those dying patterns. No one fishes it anymore, so the trout love it."

Many years ago, when I was still living in Pennsylvania, my father and I were active members of the Blair County Trout Unlimited Chapter. John Kennedy, one of the chapter's founders, had a fondness for fishing the

The Spruce Fly is representative of older streamer styles, many of which aren't popular today as anglers strive for more built-in movement in their baitfish imitations. But that doesn't mean these older flies won't work. Showing the fish something different can sometimes be the key to fishing success.

Spruce Fly. On one memorable trip to south-central Pennsylvania's Yellow Creek, Mr. Kennedy had a banner day. I don't remember the exact number of fish he caught, but I believe it was around a hundred. The Blair County TU Chapter was eventually renamed the John Kennedy Chapter due to his prowess as an angler and his extensive conservation efforts. But when I think of Mr. Kennedy, I always think of the Spruce Fly. Now, I'm not suggesting that you'll catch a hundred trout if you fish this fly in Yellowstone National Park, but anytime someone in a fly shop disappears into the store's recesses and returns with a proven fly pattern they claim is not often fished but the fish love it, you should probably take note.

Since I was given a Spruce Fly at Big Sky Anglers fly shop, I've come across it again. I bought a copy of Bruce Staples and Bob Jacklin's new book, *Fly Fishing West Yellowstone: A History and Guide* (Stackpole, 2021), and sure enough, it includes a tying recipe and a brief history for the Light Spruce Fly. After not thinking about this pattern for over twenty years, I'm taking this as a sign to throw some Spruce Flies in the park this fall.

Fishing Techniques

Michael Delfino told me that most of the anglers fishing the Spruce Fly are doing so with two-handed Spey rods. A Spey rod is an extra-long fly rod with which anglers use two hands (though single-handed Spey rods are also available) to fish waters that are too big to effectively cover with a standard fly rod. The Madison River's pools in the park are often large, and I can certainly see the advantage of using a Spey rod to fish them. But even if you're not a Spey fisher, you can still use the Spruce Fly with a standard trout rod and a floating line. You'll generally want to use a longer leader, a 9-footer, to give the fly some separation from the floating line so

it can sink. Make sure you use heavy tippet: I always begin my streamer fishing with tippet sized 0X to 2X.

If I'm fishing particularly deep pools, where the fish hold near the bottom, I'll often use a type 6 (a line that sinks approximately 6 inches per second) full-sinking or sink-tip fly line with a very short leader (around 3 feet). But most anglers will probably prefer the sink-tip line where only the tip section sinks and the rest of the line floats. This can be important for the wading fly fisher (boats are not allowed on rivers and creeks in the park) because the floating line isn't getting caught around rocks, sticks, and other subsurface debris as you strip it back to you.

If you choose a full-sinking line, you have to think about where you're placing the excess as you strip in. Most anglers wrap it in loose coils around the hand in which they are stripping, but some also use a stripping basket. The full-sinking line's advantage is that you can get your fly even deeper than you can with a sink-tip. And there's nothing better than getting deeper into Yellowstone.

John Campbell swings a streamer for lake-run brown trout in the Madison River just outside of West Yellowstone. The fall can be one of the most beautiful and pleasant times to fish the park, but it can also be snowing, windy, and miserable. Sometimes, the trout seem to prefer the nasty weather.

Index

About the Author

Paul Weamer has been a professional fly tier and designer, fly-fishing guide, and co-owner or manager of fly-fishing shops and guide services, and he is the coordinator of the Yellowstone Fly Fishing Volunteer Program. He is a contributing editor for *Fly Fisherman* magazine and the author or coauthor of several fly-fishing books. Paul lives in Paradise Valley, Montana, where he guides fly anglers on the legendary trout waters that flow through Yellowstone National Park and southwestern Montana.